ON THE EDGE OF FOREVER

History's Grand Design a

RAYMOND H. W

REVIEW AND HERALD® PUBLISHING ASSOCIATION
HAGERSTOWN, MD 21740

Texts credited to NEB are from *The New English Bible*. © The
Delegates of the Oxford University Press and the Syndics of the
Cambridge University Press 1961, 1970. Reprinted by permission.
Bible texts credited to RSV are from the Revised Standard
Version of the Bible, copyright © 1946, 1952, 1971, by the
Division of Christian Education of the National Council of the
Churches of Christ in the U.S.A. Used by permission.

This book was
Copyedited by Jocelyn Fay and Lori Halvorsen
Designed by Mark O'Connor
Cover photo from PhotoDisc
Typeset:11/12 Bembo

PRINTED IN U.S.A.

06 05 04 03 02   5 4 3 2 1

R&H Cataloging Service
Woolsey, Raymond H.
    On the edge of forever

    1. Bible–Prophecies.   I. Title.
BS647.2.W 64220.1'5 78-17936

ISBN 0-8280-1642-9

To order additional copies of *On the Edge of Forever,* by
Raymond H. Woolsey, call 1-800-765-6955.
Visit us at www.reviewandherald.com for information on
other Review and Herald products.

CONTENTS

FOOTPRINT
IN TIME

A SCRAGGLY-BEARDED man in a flowing used-to-be-white robe marches solemnly along the sidewalks of a large city. Like a protester in a demonstration, he carries on his shoulders a sign that says "Jesus Is Coming Again."

On the commons of a university campus a group of "born-again" Christians hold an outdoor rally. Full of enthusiasm, they pass out leaflets on the Second Coming to anyone who approaches.

"Yes, the church teaches the Parousia, or the Second Coming," intones a Catholic theologian. "But the subject is open to various interpretations. We'll have to wait for more definitive light on the subject."

A Protestant minister is more positive, but on a different tack: "Of course Jesus is coming. In fact, He has already come. You see, the Bible statements must be understood in a spiritual sense. Jesus comes every time a dear sinner believes on Him. He comes into the converted heart and sets up His kingdom of grace there."

A popular topic, the Second Coming. Rock musicians sing it to a heavy beat. Cocktail celebrants make jokes about it. Bible students get out their atlases of the Middle East and plot the political and military moves of nations that, according to them, presage the earthly reign of Christ.

Is there any way to winnow the wheat from the chaff on this topic? If it is true that Jesus will return to earth as a universal monarch, it is the most portentous event that faces modern humanity. Surely we cannot afford to be wrong! There may not be a second chance!

But some, even among Christians, are not enamored by the subject. They say, "God has too much to do to be bothered with this little planet. It is only a speck in an infinite universe. Why should He pay it special attention?"

That is a basic question, and it deserves first consideration. Just how much credibility is to be given, in this twenty-first-century age, to the idea that God intervenes in human affairs—much less that Jesus Christ is coming again in person? People cross continents in a few hours and think nothing of it—indeed, some do it several times a week. Soon astronauts will be heading to the planets. Computers get smaller and more diverse. There is hardly a segment of human existence that hasn't been affected by the microchip and its successors. Where is the need for God in all this?

At the same time, human horror and suffering continue apace. Thousands die in an instant in terrorist attacks on major cities. Hundreds of thousands of people are systematically exterminated by totalitarian and revolutionary governments. Diseases for which no cure has been found strike relentlessly and unselectively on young innocents, on people in their prime, and on beloved elders. Where is God when we need Him?

Is belief in the second coming of Jesus merely an escapism? Is it realistic to conceive that the world will not continue as it has? What evidence is there that a different order of events is in the offing?

Run your hand over a globe of the world. Feel any hot spots? Not on your globe, perhaps, but the world itself certainly has plenty of them. One of the hottest is in that corner where Africa joins Asia. Tensions, even war, between Arab and Israeli continue to flare, a burning fuse under a nuclear powder keg.

At the heart of the Middle East controversy is old Jerusalem, a city of sacred dimensions to Jews, Muslims, and Christians. And embedded in that city is a spot that stands as solid evidence of this fact: God interposes in the affairs of human beings!

We get so caught up in the cares of daily existence, making a living and entertaining ourselves, that we are likely to dismiss from mind the Power that rules the world. Just as we flip on our home lights with no thought of the dynamos that generate the electricity, so we live our lives from the cradle to the grave with too little attention to the energy that drives each individual cell in our bodies, or the Divine Intelligence that set this world spinning in space.

But occasionally God reveals Himself in no uncertain terms. Sometimes He steps into the stream of our existence with thunderous tread. Later we may see only His footprints, but they remind us that there is a God and that He is in ultimate control.

That hot spot in old Jerusalem seems innocuous enough. It is only a portion of a retaining wall, the only visible remains of Herod's Temple, a relic nearly 2,000 years old.

The Temple itself had been built at tremendous expense over a period of some 80 years and was a worthy monument of the Roman Empire. Six years after its completion the Romans themselves stormed and burned it, an act that was a clear fulfillment of a prophecy.

Now, there are predictions, prognostications, forecasts—and there are prophecies. There's a difference. This prophecy was direct and specific; it gave a time limit. It was made by God.

Actually, it was made by Jesus Christ. Through the process of human birth He, as God, entered the human race, and the race has never been the same since. He set into motion a certain preplanned chain of events, a line of action involving earthly and beyond-earthly powers. He outlined what those events would be, so we can judge both His own authenticity as well as His prophetic accuracy. We can check His credentials.

Herod the Great began building the Temple some 20 years before Jesus' birth. (Strictly speaking, it was a rebuilding; an earlier Temple was removed portion by portion and replaced with a much more elaborate structure.) Completion of the main shrine took eight years. Then Herod began enlarging the courts and the adjoining buildings, a project that outlasted him by several decades. The result was an edifice that rivaled Solomon's Temple.

Now, Jesus Christ was a man of His times. He walked the vast courts of that Temple. He worshiped there. He knew the veneration with which the Jews regarded the place. Even to speak disparagingly of the building was considered worthy of death. But one day Jesus told a small coterie of followers that the day would come, within their lifetime, when the Temple would be forcibly demolished—not one stone, He said, would be left upon another.

The Temple itself was not Jesus' main concern.

He knew that its true significance would end within a few days. But His disciples didn't know that. He really brought them up short with this prophecy, but He did it in order to introduce to them a subject infinitely more important, namely, the time when He personally would ring down the curtain on earth's history.

Jesus went on with some counsel about the future of Jerusalem and the Temple. Then He led them into the subject they needed to hear. "Then shall appear the sign of the Son of man in heaven, . . ." He said, "and they shall see the Son of man coming in the clouds of heaven with power and great glory" (Matthew 24:30).

About 35 years after Jesus spoke those words, the Jews revolted against Roman rule. After four years of sparring, the Romans came in force under the generalship of Titus and besieged Jerusalem. Titus gave specific orders that the Temple be spared, but, goaded by Jewish sallies, a soldier threw a firebrand through an opening, and the cedar-lined chamber burst into flames that leaped unquenched until the building was gutted.

A million Jews died in the battle. Many more were scattered to the four winds, or were carried in chains to Rome. Both Jerusalem and the Temple were razed to the ground. Of the Temple, the only portion remaining is that small section of retaining wall. For centuries Orthodox Jews have pilgrimaged to that spot to mourn the loss of their Temple and to pray for its restoration. So the place has been called the Wailing Wall.

That section of wall stands today as witness to the prophecy of Jesus: it reminds us that what He said would happen did happen. It also testifies to what He said of the future: He Himself will return. Not only does God interject Himself directly into human history at decisive moments, but He creates those moments, and He is working out a divine plan that will climax with the Son of God in uncontested control of all human destiny.

As surely as there is a Wailing Wall in Jerusalem, as surely as there is a Bible, as surely as Jesus lived on earth—as surely as there is a God in heaven!—Jesus is coming again.

Humanity lives on hope. To sustain His people through their toil and tears, Jesus told them what they could expect at the end: He would come again. Through His Spirit He would be with them in trial, and when the right time would come He would return in person, as part of the divine plan. Toward that end He instructed us to pray: "Thy kingdom come. . . . For thine is the kingdom, and the power, and the glory, for ever."

This hope has sustained the church when nothing else could. It put a spring in the steps of Paul; it put a gleam in the eye of John, an exile on Patmos; it put fortitude in the Christian martyrs in the arenas of Rome; it put daring in the Waldenses and Albigenses; it put spirit in the pen of Luther. Today it gives us purpose and a goal, a reason for living. Jesus is coming again!

A TROUBLED KING,
A DREAM EXPLAINED

WHEN JESUS outlined for His disciples the events that would culminate in the destruction of the Temple and of Jerusalem, He referred to another prophecy, made 600 years earlier, that dealt with the same situation. By studying that other prophecy, particularly in the light of Jesus' words and the events of His life, we can better understand God's role in human affairs. Especially, we can gain an insight into His ultimate plans for Planet Earth.

"When ye therefore," said Jesus, "shall see the abomination of desolation, spoken of by Daniel the prophet, stand in the holy place, (whoso readeth, let him understand:) then let them which be in Judea flee into the mountains" (Matthew 24:15, 16).

Not only does Jesus give His approval of Daniel as an authoritative speaker for God; He commands us to read and understand his words. If you haven't studied the book of Daniel lately, here is a good opportunity to do so.

Daniel was a young Jew of the princely line, taken captive by Nebuchadnezzar, king of Babylon, in an early siege of Jerusalem. Although this Nebuchadnezzar showed many of the traits of a Middle Eastern despot, he demonstrated some notable qualities of character as well. Instead of putting to the sword all royalty of the nations he subjugated, he selected the most promising young princes to help him in his rule. Thus Daniel and a few of his companions found themselves being trained to serve as the king's counselors.

One night, when Daniel was still a relative novice in matters of court, Nebuchadnezzar was startled with a demonstration of the very fact we are considering, that God intervenes in human affairs. He had a dream; it struck him so hard he awoke, and then he couldn't remember what he had dreamed.

The king's Eastern culture led him to place great importance on that dream, and he called in those who had spent their lives studying dreams and omens. They were the equivalent of today's astrologers, tea-leaf readers, and crystal-ball gazers. They were important, influential people in their society; they claimed to be in direct communication with the gods, and they had lived well off the king's treasury.

But in this time of the king's need, they failed him. They said that if he told them the dream, they could give the interpretation. But Nebuchadnezzar reasoned that if they were in communion with the gods, they should know the dream. He denounced them as rascals; they had been hoodwinking him all along, he said. He decreed that all his counselors should be executed.

When the soldiers came for Daniel in the general roundup, it was the first he knew of the situation. He asked for and was granted a royal audience. Meanwhile he prayed to God, and the Lord revealed to him what the king had dreamed, as well as the meaning of it.

"There is a God in heaven," Daniel told the monarch, "that revealeth secrets, and maketh known to the king Nebuchadnezzar what shall be in the latter days" (Daniel 2:28). Then he proceeded to recall the dream to the troubled king's mind.

The king had seen a great image of a man. The head of the image was made of gold, the breast and arms were of silver, the thighs were of brass, the legs were of iron, and the feet were partly iron and partly clay. The king in his dream saw a great stone "cut out without hands," Daniel specified. (We can almost see the king nodding his head in great excitement as the dream comes back to him once more.) The stone hit the image on the feet, and ground it to powder. Then the stone grew and grew until it filled the entire earth.

The dream having been recalled to him, the king was even more anxious to know its meaning. To have dreamed of such a dramatic occurrence and then to have lost the entire thing had been very traumatic. He was sure there was an important message in it. And there was. As Daniel had said, "God in heaven . . . maketh known to the king Nebuchadnezzar what shall be in the latter days."

Not only does God know the future—He takes direct action in shaping it. Oh, yes, people are free to make their own choices, and sometimes (too often!) this interferes with God's plans. But God is supreme and all-powerful. He so works things that eventually His will is accomplished. But how much better it is for us when we cooperate with God! To facilitate that cooperation is why God reveals to us His will, and that is also why He gives us glimpses into the future, through prophecy. That is why He gave to Nebuchadnezzar this dream. God moves not only on a universal scale, or a global scale, or a national scale; He is also directly interested in each one of us and invites us to investigate Him, to learn more and cooperate with Him.

This point was demonstrated in Daniel's life as well as in the king's. The same God who gave Nebuchadnezzar the dream gave Daniel the interpretation. This saved the lives of Daniel and his companions; further, it gave them an opportunity to witness concerning the true God to the pagan king. When we find ourselves in a difficult situation, it may be either that God is trying to get our attention to tell us something, or that He is giving us an opportunity to tell something to someone else. This personal and direct interest that God has in each one of us is evident throughout the books of Daniel and Revelation.

Daniel plunged into the interpretation of the dream as God had shown it to him. He reminded Nebuchadnezzar that it was this God who had established him on his throne and had enlarged his borders. "Thou art this head of gold," he said to Nebuchadnezzar. Nevertheless, the Babylonian dynasty would not last. Another power would arise, albeit not so opulent as Babylon, even as silver is inferior to gold. Then there would be a third world power, represented by brass, followed by another, represented by iron. Each succeeding power would be stronger and larger, yet less luxurious and magnificent.

Following the fourth kingdom there would be no single great world power. The feet of the image were of iron mingled with clay. As Daniel pointed out, iron and clay do not mix. Similarly, following that fourth power the nations of earth would be fragmented. There would be attempts at unification, but they would prove to be in vain. "They shall not cleave one to another, even as iron is not mixed with clay," declared the prophet (verse 43).

A look at history reveals how accurately yet how simply the course of world empires was portrayed in the king's dream. In the days of Nebuchadnezzar's grandson the empire of Babylon passed over to the Medes and Persians, principally the latter. The rule of Greece followed that of Persia, and then the Roman legions conquered all.

After about 600 years of rule, the Roman Empire broke up, piecemeal, as it was invaded by hordes of barbarians from the north—the Franks and the Visigoths, Vandals and Ostrogoths. These were the forerunners of today's European nations, and were represented in the dream image by the feet of iron mingled with clay.

There have been many attempts to unite the political forces that succeeded the Roman Empire. Charlemagne, the Ottomans, Napoleon Bonaparte, Kaiser Wilhelm, Adolf Hitler—all are notable examples of would-be world rulers. But their empires fell far short of those of the four great kingdoms, or died aborning. In the first decade of the twentieth century nearly every crowned head of Europe was interrelated by blood or by marriage, but that did not prevent World War I.

Endeavors have been made through important treaties and diplomatic maneuvers to accomplish what force could not do, but Europe today remains splintered. The European Union has been only partially successful. Even now serious attempts are being made toward a Pan-European Parliament. King Nebuchadnezzar's dream of feet of iron and clay, and Daniel's interpretation, are as fresh as today's newspaper. We are living, as it were, in the feet of the image.

But what of that stone that smote the great image? What is the windup of this prophecy?

Daniel said that the stone represented yet another kingdom. But it was "cut out without hands," indicating that this kingdom would be of different origin than the others. Moreover, it became far more universal and was "everlasting."

The stone struck the image on the feet, that part representing the period when the nations of earth would be fragmented. "In the days of these kings," said Daniel, "shall the God of heaven set up a kingdom, which shall never be destroyed: and the kingdom shall not be left to other people, but it shall break in pieces and consume all these kingdoms, and it shall stand for ever" (verse 44).

Here, in just so many words, God announced that history will not continue on in the hands of human beings. The day is coming when God will sweep aside human political intentions and establish His own reign on earth, and it will be an everlasting reign. It will not be just another earthly kingdom or nation, one that happens to have God's particular approval. The stone represents the time when God will rule earth, directly and in person. That is the way it was in the Garden of Eden before Adam and Eve sinned. The goal of history, the purpose of God, is that He shall restore His rulership.

But God's kingdom will not be one of force. He is not like that. This will be a kingdom characterized by love. And God's love for His subjects will be reflected in the love of each of them for Him.

Christ's first advent was a major step toward the establishment of that kingdom. He kept speaking about it while He was on earth, describing what it was like and who would have a part in it. He indicated it would be in two phases. The first is when we acknowledge Him as king in our hearts and lives. "The kingdom of God is within you," He said (Luke 17:21).

The second phase of Christ's universal reign is when all sin and rebellion have been forever overthrown and He reigns unopposed throughout all the earth. He will be here in person, visible. It was to this second phase of His kingdom that Jesus referred in His Olivet discourse when He told His disciples, "Then shall the King say unto them on his right hand, Come, ye blessed of my Father, inherit the kingdom prepared for you from the foundation of the world" (Matthew 25:34).

The cutting out of the stone, then, and its striking the image on the feet, apply to the second coming of Jesus. The indication is that that event will be in our day. Let us establish Jesus as king in our hearts now, so that when He comes in power and glory we may be accounted worthy to be citizens of His eternal kingdom.

THE THRONE BEHIND
ALL THRONES

NEBUCHADNEZZAR WAS greatly impressed with Daniel's ability to recall his dream and to give the interpretation. He honored Daniel's God, who had spoken through the young man, and he honored Daniel. He made Daniel chief of the headquarters province of Babylon, and set him over all the other counselors of the realm.

But the pagan king was not yet ready to acknowledge God's ultimate supremacy in the affairs of earth, much less in his own life. After some reflection he decided to challenge the dream. Instead of being merely the golden head of an image that bespoke succeeding kingdoms, Nebuchadnezzar wanted to be the whole thing. He wanted his dynasty to last forever. He would build an image that was all of gold.

Nebuchadnezzar built his image and set it up in a great plain. He then called in all his princes and rulers, those who represented him in the far corners of his empire. They were all commanded to worship the golden image, with death decreed for the one who defied the king. He would root out anyone who threatened his universal authority and the perpetuity of his reign.

But three young men, friends of Daniel, who had trained with him and who had been given positions of responsibility, refused to worship the image. They were loyal to the king in all other respects, but they could not worship anyone or anything other than the God of heaven. Nebuchadnezzar ordered them bound and thrown into fiery ovens specially super-heated for the purpose.

The fires were so hot that the men detailed to throw in the Hebrews were killed instantly, but the three faithful ones themselves were not hurt. The king looked into the flames and saw that their bonds had burned and that they were walking around freely inside the furnace. In fact, there was a fourth Person with them. The king understood that their God was protecting them. Again he acknowledged that the God of heaven is more powerful than any earthly power. Their God had "changed the king's word," he said (Daniel 3:28).

Once more the king had a dream. This time, ap-parently, he did not forget what he saw in the night, but he had just as much trouble getting a meaning from his astrologers and magicians as he had the first time. Certainly they did their best at supplying an in-terpretation, for their livelihoods, if not their lives, were at stake. But the king was not satisfied. Perhaps he tested them by giving them the dream individually and found that they did not agree with each other as to the interpretation. Perhaps they somehow recog-nized behind the dream a Power with which they as pagans were not familiar. In any event they once again failed the king.

Then Nebuchadnezzar called in Daniel, probably

feeling he should have called him in the first place. In this dream, the king said, he had seen a great tree. "The height thereof reached unto heaven," he recalled, "and the sight thereof to the end of all the earth" (Daniel 4:11). The tree bore food enough for all creatures, and its branches sheltered all life.

In his dream the king saw further that an angel came down from heaven bearing the decree that the tree was to be cut down. Only a stump was to be left, and that was to be bound about with a band of iron and a band of brass. What the angel said next must surely have puzzled the king: "Let his heart be changed from man's [Did the tree, then, represent a person?], and let a beast's heart be given unto him; and let seven times pass over him. This matter is by the decree of the watchers, and the demand by the word of the holy ones: to the intent that the living may know that the most High ruleth in the kingdom of men, and giveth it to whomsoever he will, and setteth up over it the basest of men" (verses 16, 17).

When the king had finished, he asked Daniel for the meaning. But Daniel was speechless. Not that he did not know the interpretation; he knew it all too well, and it bode ill for the king. Finally, with the king's encouragement, Daniel began revealing to Nebuchadnezzar the meaning of the dream.

"The tree that thou sawest, . . . it is thou, O king" (verses 20-22). Nebuchadnezzar had grown so great and powerful that his kingdom encompassed practically all the known world. But the decree of the angel was against the king: "They shall drive thee from men, and thy dwelling shall be with the beasts of the field, and they shall make thee to eat grass as oxen" (verse 25). For seven years the great Nebuchadnezzar was to live as an animal of the field.

But Daniel went beyond the literal interpretation of the dream. He saw that this message was a warning from the God of heaven that the king was becoming too proud. If he voluntarily humbled himself and recognized the power of God as his ally instead of taking all glory to himself, he might be spared the degradation decreed against him. This was Daniel's counsel to Nebuchadnezzar.

Perhaps for a while the stark message had its effect on the king's heart. But about a year later he was walking about in his palace, priding himself on the majesty that had accrued to him and that he credited to his own prowess and wisdom. Suddenly he heard a voice from heaven repeat the words of the dream and of Daniel's interpretation: "The kingdom is departed from thee. And they shall drive thee from men, and thy dwelling shall be with the beasts of the field" (verses 31, 32).

The words were fulfilled within the hour. The king suddenly lost his reason. With it he lost his throne and his place among civilized people. He lived outdoors like an animal. His nails grew out like a bird's claws, and his body hair grew long like that of a creature of the wild. Thus he existed for seven long years.

At length Nebuchadnezzar's reason returned to him. He recognized what had happened, and why. He had learned his painful lesson. "Now," he said, "I Nebuchadnezzar praise and extol and honour the King of heaven, all whose works are truth, and his ways judgment: and those that walk in pride he is able to abase" (verse 37).

One would think that upon the king's losing his reason, another would take over his throne and after seven years be so firmly entrenched that Nebuchadnezzar would not be able to regain it. Many a throne has been lost over much less. But again the Lord's hand is revealed. After so long a period of living the life of an animal, Nebuchadnezzar's dominion was restored to him. "Mine honour and brightness returned unto me; and my counsellors and my lords sought unto me; and I was established in my kingdom, and excellent majesty was added unto me" (verse 36). Thus was demonstrated the words Nebuchadnezzar had heard in his dream: "To the intent that the living may know that the most High ruleth in the kingdom of men, and giveth it to whomsoever he will." From this time forward Nebuchadnezzar was a worshiper of the true God.

How merciful God is to humanity, to us today no less than to the pagan despot in Daniel's day. We may be agnostics, or even atheists, or perhaps nominal Christians bent on having our own way. "But God commendeth his love toward us, in that, while we were yet sinners, Christ died for us" (Romans 5:8).

But Christ's great sacrifice is a waste of effort where we are concerned if we ignore or reject it. As He loves us personally and died to save us individually, so we must individually accept Him as our personal Savior.

Nebuchadnezzar's successors did not learn from his experience. King Belshazzar was having a great feast one night in the palace beside the Euphrates. A thousand of his lords were sharing the festivities with him. Little did they care that an enemy army was besieging the city. They trusted to the strength of their walls and to the defenses at the gates that guarded the river as it ran through the city. This was the city Belshazzar's predecessor had built, the greatest city in the world. It held enough supplies to hold off any army indefinitely.

In his drunken revelry Belshazzar called for the

sacred vessels that had been confiscated from the Temple at Jerusalem. He wanted to drink from these as a symbolic gesture of defiance against heaven. He failed to remember Nebuchadnezzar's dream, the one about the great image. Although Babylon was represented by the head of gold, it was to be followed by another kingdom, of silver. Little did Belshazzar know that it was the armies of that "silver" kingdom that stood just outside his walls.

While he was drinking, his dulled eyes were arrested by a startling sight. Instantly he sobered. A bodyless hand was writing in letters of fire on the wall of the banquet hall. Even after the hand disappeared, the letters continued to burn into the king's consciousness. He sent for his counselors, but as so many times in the past, when it came to interpreting what really mattered they were helpless. At last the queen mother remembered Daniel, now an old man, and advised Belshazzar to call on his services.

When Daniel arrived, he reminded the king of how marvelously the God of heaven had revealed Himself to Nebuchadnezzar. That monarch had learned his true relationship toward God. Belshazzar might have profited from the same lesson; instead, he had acted as if there were no God. Now the Lord had revealed Himself in no uncertain terms. We do not know in what language the four words on the wall were written. Daniel read them in Aramaic, a language well known to the king. They may indeed have been in that language, but they were nevertheless so cryptic that they needed an interpretation. This Daniel proceeded to give.

Mene, "numbered," was the first word, and it was repeated for emphasis. "God hath numbered thy kingdom," Daniel said, "and finished it" (Daniel

5:26). *Tekel,* "weighed": "Thou art weighed in the balances, and art found wanting" (verse 27). *Upharsin* (or *peres,* another form of the same word), "pieces": "Thy kingdom is divided," broken into pieces (verse 28). That very night Cyrus, general of that army outside the wall, found a way to breach the defenses. He swept into the city and slew Belshazzar. The "silver" kingdom had replaced the "gold."

There is an interesting corollary of this victory of Cyrus over Belshazzar. Cyrus had gained his advantage by an ingenious strategy. He knew that the walls of the city were impregnable. He also knew that the river Euphrates ran through the city and that the street gates along the river were usually guarded. Upriver from the city he diverted the water into an artificial lake. When the river level at the city dropped, Cyrus was able to slip his army through unguarded river gates and into the palace. The palace guards probably were slack in their responsibility, in part because of their trust in their embattlements and in part because of the revelry in the banquet hall.

The most interesting aspect is that this ruse had been foretold a hundred years beforehand, and its architect had been called by name. The prophet Isaiah had written, "Thus saith the Lord to his anointed, to Cyrus, whose right hand I have holden, to subdue nations before him; and I will loose the loins of kings, to open before him the two leaved gates; and the gates shall not be shut; I will go before thee . . . I will give thee the treasures of darkness, and hidden riches of secret places, that thou mayest know that I, the Lord, which call thee by thy name, am the God of Israel" (Isaiah 45:1-3).

How could anyone doubt that God is the unseen power above and beyond the kingdoms and nations of earth? This is not to say that He is to be blamed for all the evil perpetrated by rulers and nations. This world is still very much in the hands of the "prince of the power of the air" (Ephesians 2:2), that is, the devil. But God's power is greater, and His will is infinite. In the overall scheme of things, He is working out His way; in the end His plan will triumph.

After Cyrus had been established upon the Persian throne, with Babylon conquered, Daniel showed him Isaiah's prophecy. That God had foretold of the exploits of Cyrus before he was even born impressed the king greatly, so much so that he treated Daniel's exiled people with favor and made arrangements for their return to their homeland in Judea.

One more king was to learn the divine omnipotence of Daniel's God. Cyrus, the Persian, was assisted in his conquests against the Babylonians by the Medes. Before Cyrus himself came to the throne, the kingdom was ruled briefly by a Mede, Darius. Daniel was made a chief counselor in the Median court, even as he had been in the Babylonian and later would be in the Persian. (Surely the hand of God was on him, that he could successfully weather first the Babylonian capture of his own city of Jerusalem, then the change from Babylonian to Median rule, and finally from Median to Persian. Although the Medes and Persians were partners, there was bound to be considerable intrigue at court. An officer of a conquered nation, and a member of a subject race at that, would normally not be allowed to live long, much less be retained at the highest level of government.)

It was during Darius's reign that Daniel had his encounter with the lions. It came about this way: The high regard in which the king held the Jew was resented by the latter's fellow counselors. They plotted his destruction. Noting that Daniel faithfully prayed every day, they tricked Darius into signing a decree that for a period of 30 days no one was to pray to any but the king. These men trusted in a very strict principle that undergirded their national system of jurisprudence: no law, once promulgated, was to be changed—ever, for any reason. Such a stricture seems a bit arrogant to us in the twenty-first century, and unwise. Nevertheless, that is the way it was in the government of the Medes and the Persians.

After King Darius had signed the law, and when he was told that Daniel had disregarded it, he knew instantly that he had been duped at the expense of his friend. Feverishly he drove his lawyers in a search for a legal loophole whereby he might save Daniel from the prescribed judgment—death in the lions' den. But it was in vain. The conspirators had drawn up their law too well, and with the king's signature on it there was no way out. Sadly Darius ordered Daniel to be cast into the den of lions.

But Darius was about to learn the lesson that Nebuchadnezzar and Belshazzar had learned, that there is a God in heaven who is greater than any earthly king, power, or law. After a sleepless and guilt-ridden night, Darius personally visited the mouth of the lions' den. And he personally heard and saw the evidence of how God had vindicated His faithful servant, in spite of the "unchangeable" laws of the Medes and Persians! God had stopped the lions' mouths so that they had not hurt Daniel. But God did not see fit to stop those mouths when the conspirators themselves were cast among the lions!

This experience of Daniel's was a microcosm of the message of his entire book: God's affairs in general, and His people in particular, are downtrodden and oppressed by the devil. But God will prevail. He will deliver His people not only from the guilt of sin but also from its power. Evil will be overcome— moreover, it will be abolished, and God's people will reign with Him in peace and righteousness.

Here is hope for you and me. Are you oppressed, discouraged? Are you worried about world-wide terroism? Perhaps you have lived a dissolute life and seek victory over sin. Perhaps you are the only Christian in your family and you find the going hard. In Christ is victory. Put yourself on His side, and you will overcome as He did, for His strength is yours. He has promised it, and in Daniel's case, as in so many others, He has proved that He keeps His promises. He gives us the power when we ascribe to Him the glory.

FOUR BEASTS
AND A JUDGMENT

THE FIRST six of the 12 chapters in the book of Daniel are narrative in style; the last six deal entirely with visions. Although two important dreams are related in the first half of the book, they did not come directly to the prophet; he served as interpreter only. The last half of the book is all his.

The first six chapters, the ones we have already surveyed, are important for several reasons. In his own visions Daniel would be witnessing the rise and fall of many nations. The events and insights recorded in these first six chapters would give him (as they give to us who study his visions) the proper perspective in which to see them. They establish the One who is in ultimate control of affairs on earth; they testify to the surety of the outcome of the visions. They demonstrate how God reaches individuals and saves them from sin.

Further, the events of these first six chapters establish Daniel's credentials as a prophet. Great and far-reaching events were to be chronicled by his pen; Daniel himself was to write with confidence, and those who studied his works were to recognize their divine origin.

In spite of the apparent dichotomy, the theme of the last half of the book is the same as that of the first half—God will have His way in the affairs of earth. Christ and His followers will have full victory over all the forces of evil. Toward that end Christ takes a personal interest in each one of us.

All of the three visions that Daniel records in chapters 7 through 12 are enlargements upon the dream that he revealed to and interpreted for King Nebuchadnezzar, recorded in the second chapter. The nature of that enlargement, and the progressive lesson that each vision brings out, will be seen as we proceed.

The first of the prophet's visions came to him during the final years of Babylon's glory, while Belshazzar was on the throne, a coregent with his father, Nabonidus. This was a period when Daniel himself was retired from the limelight of state affairs, though he later was again placed in positions of prominence. Now he had opportunity to reflect upon God's place in the affairs of humanity. He was particularly concerned about the fate of his own people, the Jews, captives in a pagan land.

In his vision Daniel saw the wind blowing upon the sea. While he watched, a great animal came up out of the sea onto the shore. The animal resembled a lion, but had eagle's wings. Soon these were plucked, and the lion took on the aspects of a man.

Then in his dream another animal followed, coming up out of the sea as did the first. This one was like a bear, and was holding three ribs in its teeth. In his vision, Daniel heard a command given to the bear to "devour much flesh" (Daniel 7:5).

A third beast arose dripping from the turbulent

waves. Somewhat similar to a leopard in general appearance, it had four wings and even four heads.

While Daniel considered these three animals, another appeared. This one was beyond comparison with any animal known to the prophet. He could describe it only as "dreadful and terrible, and strong exceedingly; and it had great iron teeth; it devoured and brake in pieces, and stamped the residue with the feet of it" (verse 7).

This fourth beast had 10 horns on its great head. Even while Daniel watched, he saw another little horn work its way up among the 10. In fact, in its upward thrust it rooted out three of the first horns. It grew more stout than any of the 10, and developed eyes and a mouth like a man's. To the prophet's consternation, the mouth began to speak "great things," blasphemies against God.

Then the setting of the vision shifted; Daniel seemed to find himself in the throne room of Deity. One whom Daniel took to be God Himself sat in judgment. Myriads of angels were in attendance; record books were opened, and the Divine One decreed that the fourth beast with its blaspheming horn should be destroyed, "given to the burning flame" (verse 11).

Daniel watched, and "one like the Son of man came with the clouds of heaven. . . . And there was given him dominion, and glory, and a kingdom, that all people, nations, and languages, should serve him: his dominion is an everlasting dominion, which shall not pass away" (verses 13, 14).

The prophet was puzzled over the meaning of what he had seen. While yet in vision he approached "one of them that stood by," apparently one of the holy angels assisting in the judgment. Daniel asked

30

him for an interpretation and, fortunately for us, he recorded what the angel said.

"These great beasts," began the angel, "which are four, are four kings, which shall arise out of the earth" (verse 17). Actually, we should understand these as four kingdoms, based on the angel's words of Daniel 7:23 and 24. Similarly, the sea from which the animals arose may be identified, from Revelation 17:15, as the total mass of peoples of earth, the sea of humanity. This little detail may not have been revealed to Daniel, or he may have chosen not to record it. In any event, it is an example of how we may gain a deeper insight into prophecy by comparing one prophecy with another. Isaiah had been instructed that the people were to be instructed "precept . . . upon precept, precept upon precept; line upon line, line upon line; here a little, and there a little" (Isaiah 28:10).

This is not to say that we are at liberty to build our own interpretations of Bible prophecy, or that we may indiscriminately mix symbols and metaphors. "No prophecy of the scripture is of any private interpretation," said the apostle Peter (2 Peter 1:20). Even as the Bible was written under the inspiration of the Holy Spirit, we should seek His guidance in its study. We should try to determine what the Bible writers intended to say, rather than color their words with our own preconceived ideas. The Bible is its own best interpreter.

"The fourth beast shall be the fourth kingdom upon earth," the angel told Daniel (Daniel 7:23). Thus we understand that the first beast, the one like a lion, represented the political power that ruled the world during Daniel's own time. That power was Babylon. In recent times significant portions of Babylon's magnificent Ishtar Gate have been unearthed, and it was found that lions with eagles' wings were used as decorations on it. Just as a lion represents Britain today, and a bear represents Russia, and an eagle represents the United States of America, so God used animals to depict nations in Daniel's vision.

Babylon started out as a great and noble power, but at the death of Nebuchadnezzar it lost its stature. The "lion" became weak.

Persia, with the Medes as allies, followed on the world scene. The three ribs that Daniel saw in the bear's mouth may well represent the three chief powers that were conquered by the Medo-Persian Empire—Babylon, Lydia, and Egypt.

After some 200 years of Persian dominance, Philip of Macedon began amalgamating the city-states of Greece. He was succeeded by his son, Alexander, who set his sights on conquering the Persian Empire and establishing his own. In 334 B.C. he crossed the Hellespont with a few thousand soldiers and a handful of supplies. Less than 10 years later he was the ruler of everything from the Adriatic Sea to the Indus River. Surely the symbol of wings is well applied to the swiftness of his world conquest.

But Alexander did not live long; he died of a fever at the age of 32. For a few years his generals tried to maintain the semblance of unity, first under Alexander's weak-minded half brother, then under Alexander's infant son. But, these efforts failing, the empire was divided among four of the conqueror's chief generals—Ptolemy, Cassander, Lysimachus, and Seleucus (later Lysimachus's territory was largely taken over by the Seleucid faction).

Though the land was divided politically, this period was essentially Greek, for the Greek influence in language, thought, and civilization prevailed. Alexander's empire was, for practical purposes, still in effect.

Thus far Daniel's vision closely parallels the dream of Nebuchadnezzar. The two close on the same note, as well. Nebuchadnezzar saw a great stone strike the image in his dream. The stone, Daniel had told him, represented a universal, everlasting kingdom that the God of heaven would set up. Similarly, in his vision Daniel saw that God would establish a kingdom wherein all nations of earth would serve Him, a dominion that would never pass away.

However, this vision goes further than the king's dream in two important respects. It gives more detail concerning the fourth kingdom (for reasons that will be brought out later in this study), and it identifies the kingdom that God will set up. It is the kingdom that will be given to "the Son of man," or Christ. Jesus Himself referred to it this way: "When the Son of man shall come in his glory, and all the holy angels with him, then shall he sit upon the throne of his glory: and before him shall be gathered all nations" (Matthew 25:31, 32).

But first there would transpire the power represented by the fourth beast, with that eleventh "little horn," which would uproot three other horns and have eyes and a mouth, and speak great things against God. Herein is the difference between Nebuchadnezzar's dream and Daniel's vision. Nebuchadnezzar was interested in political affairs: Would his dynasty be a lasting one? God gave him his answer in political terms. Daniel, on the other hand, was more interested in religious matters: What did the future hold for the people of God? His vision answered that, in part.

It was the fourth beast in his vision that troubled Daniel the most, and he asked the angel about it particularly. The angel said it was the fourth kingdom. It will, he said, "devour the whole earth, and shall tread it down, and break it in pieces" (Daniel 7:23). The power that subdued the Greeks, of course, was Rome, represented by the iron legs of Nebuchadnezzar's image. The world had never seen so dominating a force. Not only did it swallow up the empire that had been Greek; it extended its iron fist to the isles of the Celts and to the forests of Germany.

"And the ten horns out of this kingdom," said the angel, "are ten kings that shall arise" (verse 24). Roman rule lasted longer than any that preceded it. It instituted civil codes that undergird jurisprudence in most of today's Western world; its engineering feats are studied and marveled over by today's architects. But eventually, through external pressures and internal dissolution, Rome's power began to wane.

Little by little, barbarian tribes from the north and northeast began to whittle away at the domain of the Caesars. As many as 20 tribes have been identified in this disintegration process, but generally 10 are named as chief: the Ostrogoths, Visigoths, Franks, Vandals, Suevi, Alamanni, Anglo-Saxons, Heruli, Lombards, and the Burgundians. Here, then, are the 10 horns of the fourth beast.

It was among these 10 horns that the eleventh, "little," horn arose. He "shall rise after them; and he shall be diverse from the first, and he shall subdue three kings. And he shall speak great words against the most High, and shall wear out the saints of the most High, and think to change times and laws: and they shall be given into his hand until a time and times and the dividing of time" (verses 24, 25).

The power that came on the world scene upon the demise of the Roman Empire, indeed, that outdid in influence any of the political successors to that kingdom, was the Papacy. For some hundreds of years the bishop of the church at Rome had been growing in influence among his fellow bishops. When the emperor moved his seat to Constantinople, it created a power vacuum that the bishop of Rome was quick to capitalize upon. Eventually Emperor Justinian decreed the Roman bishop "head of all the holy churches" and "head of all the holy priests of God."

In the meantime, the territory of the empire and the city of Rome itself was feeling the weight of the barbarian kings. Nominally Christian but Arian by persuasion, as opposed to Catholicism, they posed a threat to the Roman bishop. One by one the three chief offenders, the Heruli, the Vandals, and the Ostrogoths, lost their power through fighting each other and finally by direct intervention from Justinian himself. The last of the three, the Ostrogoths, were driven from Rome in A.D. 538.

In eight distinct points in these two verses of Daniel 7 (24 and 25), the "little horn" is identified as the Papacy: (a) it arose within the territory of the Roman Empire; (b) it arose after the breakup of that empire; (c) it was different in nature from the "ten kingdoms" (wherein they were political, the Papacy was a combination of religious and political power); (d) three of the first kings were subdued in its rise; (e) it spake "great words against the most High," in calling the pope the "vicegerent of God on earth," with power to forgive sins and even to cast down angels from heaven if need be; (f) it persecuted Christians, arranging for the deaths of millions who dared to believe differently from the church's decrees; (g) it tried to change times and laws, claiming that the church had power to alter the Ten Commandments, wherein image worship is forbidden (the second commandment) and the seventh day is decreed as the day of worship (the fourth commandment—the papal church claims responsibility for shifting allegiance to Sunday); (h) it maintained its religio-political hegemony for 1,260 years.

This last point needs a bit of explanation. In his vision Daniel learned that the little horn was to exercise power for "a time and times and the dividing of time." This is more properly translated in the Revised Standard Version as "time, two times, and half a time." From Daniel 4:23 we understand that the Aramaic word translated "time" actually means a year. By comparing the verses in Daniel 7 with Revelation 12:14 and 6, and with Revelation 11:2 and 3, we discover that three and one-half "times," or prophetic years, are equated with 1,260 prophetic days, which are equated with 42 prophetic months. Thus a prophetic year equals 360 prophetic days, or 12 30-day prophetic months. Numbers 14:34 and Ezekiel 4:6 illustrate that a prophetic day is equal to a literal year. And so the little horn's "time and times and the dividing of time," or three and one-half prophetic years, is 1,260 literal years. Counting from A.D. 538, when Justinian's decree on behalf of the pope became effective, 1,260 years extends to A.D. 1798—the very year when the French general Berthier, upon Napoleon's orders, entered Rome with an army, arrested the pope, and carried him away to exile in France!

(At this juncture we should make clear that the prophecy is not a denunciation of Roman Catholics per se. God has candidates for His kingdom in that persuasion as assuredly as in any other. God neither saves nor condemns according to our church affiliation but according to our personal relationship with Him. Says Christ, "Not every one that saith unto me,

Lord, Lord, shall enter into the kingdom of heaven; but he that doeth the will of my Father which is in heaven" [Matthew 7:21]. But God does point the finger of judgment at the papal system because of its attitude toward His law, His salvation ministry, and His faithful followers. And, as we shall see in our study of Revelation, apostate Protestantism comes under the same condemnation.)

With the chief elements of Daniel's vision identified, we can now address ourselves to its main import. According to the space given to them in the vision and the interpretation, the first three kingdoms, or even the fourth, are not the most important aspects of the vision. Rather, it was during the period of that little horn, while it was "speaking great things," that Daniel saw some dramatic events transpire:

First, thrones were "cast down," or set up, according to other translations (the sense is that a judicial event is about to take place). Then the "Ancient of days," or God the Father, sat on His throne (Daniel 7:9). Daniel tries to describe God here, but remember that what he saw was only a representation of God, for as Jesus said, no human has seen the Father; only "he which is God, he hath seen the Father" (John 6:46).

"Thousand thousands ministered unto him, and ten thousand times ten thousand stood before him" (Daniel 7:10). There is no numbering of the myriad angels who attend God and who are ready to do His bidding in the far corners of His vast universe.

"The judgment was set," the record continues, "and the books were opened." Daniel was witnessing the great judgment day, which was still future in his time. It was still future in Paul's time, for he reasoned with Governor Felix of "judgment to come" (Acts

24:25). This is the judgment for which the evil angels are held (2 Peter 2:4), and in which all shall be judged, both the living and the dead (2 Timothy 4:1), the righteous and the wicked (Ecclesiastes 3:17).

The great standard in this judgment, by which all shall be measured, is the Ten Commandments, the law of God. "Fear God, and keep his commandments: for this is the whole duty of man. For God shall bring every work into judgment, with every secret thing, whether it be good, or whether it be evil" (Ecclesiastes 12:13, 14).

As evidence in this great trial, God brings forth books wherein are recorded our every thought, deed, and word. Whether these are books such as we know is beside the point; God has His own way of doing things. These records are called variously "the book of the living" (Psalm 69:28), "the Lamb's book of life" (Revelation 21:27), "the book of life" (Revelation 3:5), and the "book of remembrance" (Malachi 3:16).

One should not conclude from this description of the judgment that God is vengefully waiting to pounce on our every word, hoping to trap us in sin. On the contrary, He is "longsuffering to us-ward, not willing that any should perish, but that all should come to repentance" (2 Peter 3:9). The fact of the matter is that there are some who claim to be loyal to God but who are actually working against Him. The judgment, then, is simply to determine who is truly on God's side. God will search the thoughts and the motives of the heart and the things done in secret, not only the public profession.

Everyone, of course, is a sinner. If only our sins are taken into account in the judgment, then no one has a chance. But we are told, "If we confess our sins, he is faithful and just to forgive us our sins, and to cleanse us from all unrighteousness. . . . And if any man sin, we have an advocate with the Father, Jesus Christ the righteous" (1 John 1:9 to 2:1). If we confess our sins, Christ forgives us of guilt. He takes our sins upon Himself as our great high priest. His death atones for them, and we are free of condemnation. In the great judgment the records will reveal who has fled to Christ for this forgiveness. Such a one will stand with a clean slate, for all his sins will have been blotted from the books.

We have in this chapter of Daniel the outline of the great controversy of the ages. From his beginning Satan has accused God of injustice, of having a law that no one could keep. He has tried to set himself up in God's stead, taking by deception the allegiance of God's creatures. This deception reaches right into the so-called Christian church—there are those who call themselves Christians who practice the methods and hold to the principles of the enemy of God.

The apostle Paul amplified this point. He revealed that before Christ returned, an apostasy would develop within the church. He described this movement as the "man of sin . . . who opposeth and exalteth himself above all that is called God, or that is worshipped; so that he as God sitteth in the temple of God, shewing himself that he is God" (2 Thessalonians 2:3, 4).

Here is a so-called Christian power that usurps the divine perquisites. Would not a church whose head claims to be God on earth, who claims to have the power to forgive sins, to be able to create the body of Christ out of a wafer of bread, fulfill the words of Paul?

The apostle continues, "Then shall that Wicked be revealed, whom the Lord shall consume with the spirit of his mouth, and shall destroy with the brightness of his coming" (verse 8). This harmonizes with the words of Gabriel to Daniel: "He shall also stand up against the Prince of princes; but he shall be broken without hand" (Daniel 8:25). No human hand will prevail against this power, but it shall meet its end when Christ comes.

God's purpose is to vindicate His character, which has been called into question; to reveal Satan for the liar that he is; and to rid the universe of Satan and all who align themselves with him. This is what the great judgment is for, to strip away all pretense and reveal the true facts in each person's case. It is in this connection that Daniel witnessed the judgment in his vision. The little horn was claiming to represent God's interests on earth, yet was all the while carrying out Satan's purposes. This great controversy, its ramifications and its outcome, is the theme of the rest of the book of Daniel and of most of the theme of its companion book, Revelation, which we shall explore later.

What happens to the little horn? "The judgment shall sit, and they shall take away his dominion, to consume and to destroy it unto the end" (Daniel 7:26). Then it is that "the Son of man came with the clouds of heaven, and came to the Ancient of days. . . . And there was given him dominion, and glory, and a kingdom, that all people, nations, and languages, should serve him" (verses 13, 14). This is an everlasting kingdom, "which shall not be destroyed" (verse 14). And the Son of man turns to His people, those who have been faithful in spite of the persecution of the little horn power, and He shares His kingdom with them: "And the kingdom and dominion, and the greatness of the kingdom under the whole heaven, shall be given to the people of the saints of the most High" (verse 27). Or, as Jesus worded it to His disciples on the Mount of Olives: "Then shall the

King say unto them on his right hand, Come, ye blessed of my Father, inherit the kingdom prepared for you from the foundation of the world" (Matthew 25:34).

Note that the investigative phase of the judgment, when the books are examined and the decision is made as to who is guilty and who is innocent, takes place before the Son of man takes His kingdom. Just as in a court of law, the passing of sentence is an important moment, but even more crucial is the decision of guilt or innocence. It would be naive to assume that we have a thousand years after Jesus' coming in which to make our lives right. Even the moment of His coming will be too late for this; our cases will already have been decided. Surely "now is the day of salvation" (2 Corinthians 6:2).

When Christ invites His people into His kingdom, it will be the fulfillment of the plan God had for human beings when He made them and put them in the Garden of Eden. They were was to have eternal life and to possess the earth as their dominion. But they forfeited those benefits; by sinning they passed the dominion of earth over to the adversary, Satan. Through His death Jesus won back the dominion. When Satan is destroyed, Jesus will be reestablished in His kingdom, and He will share it with His faithful ones. Such is the glorious plan of God, and you and I are its benefactors. He had you and me in mind when He went to Calvary. God grant that He will have you and me in mind when He returns to make up His kingdom!

CHRIST AND THE COUNTDOWN

A COUPLE of years after his first vision, Daniel had another. It was in connection with this vision and its fulfillment that Jesus referred to Daniel some 600 years later.

Once again Daniel saw animals. This time a great ram was "pushing westward, and northward, and southward; so that no beasts might stand before him" (Daniel 8:4). Quite evidently this power began its conquest from the east. But although he "did according to his will, and became great," another animal suddenly appeared, coming from the west. This was a goat, moving so fast it didn't seem to be touching the ground. The goat bore a "notable horn" between his eyes, (verse 5).

While Daniel watched, the goat ran into the ram, knocked him down, and trampled on him. Presently the goat's great horn was broken, and four more came up in its place. Then Daniel saw another "little horn," which became "exceeding great" (verse 9). Not only did it persecute the people of God; it boasted itself against God Himself. It desecrated the sanctuary of

God and took away the daily sacrifices. Moreover, Daniel heard that this situation would prevail for "two thousand and three hundred days" (verse 14).

Daniel was as puzzled about this, as you or I would be. But God, who was giving him the vision, wanted him to understand its meaning. None less than Gabriel, the angel who stands in the presence of God, was commissioned to interpret the vision to the prophet.

"The ram which thou sawest having two horns are the kings of Media and Persia. And the rough goat is the king of Grecia," Gabriel explained (verses 20, 21). This vision also, then, is of the rise and fall of nations. But it is concerned with more than that. Each succeeding vision, while going over the same ground, that is, giving a prehistory of political events, goes progressively deeper into the details of history's climax. First King Nebuchadnezzar saw four great world powers, followed by a period of "iron mixed with miry clay," during which "the God of heaven set up a kingdom." Daniel's first vision added the details of a religious power that would blaspheme God, persecute His people, and try to change His law. Further, the kingdom that God would set up was identified as the one over which Christ would be the king.

Now Daniel is led over the same ground again. Let us note the details this vision brings to light. Babylon is no longer in the picture. Although the vision was given during the reign of Belshazzar, Babylon's remaining time was so short that it did not figure in the vision. Instead, Daniel is introduced to the ram, which represented Media and Persia.

Here also is a difference, a progression over the previous revelations. The power represented by the animal is called by name. No room is allowed for guessing, for private interpretations. No wonder

Daniel could be so certain, when called to translate the handwriting on the wall of Belshazzar's feast, that the kingdom had passed to the Medes and Persians.

And the goat is named just as clearly—Greece—and its great horn is identified as Greece's "first king." This would be Alexander the Great, who brought Persia to its knees and conquered to the Indus River. When the horn was broken, that is, when Alexander died, control of the empire passed to four generals, as was noted in the previous chapter.

Now comes the part that elaborates on the vision of chapter 7, even as that vision elaborated on the king's dream of the great metallic image.

"In the latter time" of the four divisions of Greek power, a "king of fierce countenance, and understanding dark sentences, shall stand up" (Daniel 8:23). The empire of Greece was followed, of course, by Rome. And in this vision the course of pagan, political Rome is of a piece with papal, ecclesiastical Rome. It was pagan Rome, through Pilate and his minions, who crucified Jesus. It was pagan Rome, in the form of Titus and his army, that burned the Temple and razed it, scattering the Jews abroad. It was papal Rome that supplanted Jesus as the only mediator between man and God, that substituted another priesthood for the relationship Christ would have with His people, that sacrifices the Son of God afresh daily in its religious services.

As a loyal and faithful Jew, Daniel was concerned for the integrity of the Lord's house and for His worship. "How long," he asked, "shall be the vision concerning the daily sacrifice, and the transgression of desolation, to give both the sanctuary and the host to be trodden under foot?" (verse 13). The answer came: "Unto two thousand and three hundred days; then shall the sanctuary be cleansed" (verse 14). The word translated "cleansed" here is also translated "justified" or "set right." However, Gabriel immediately told Daniel that the vision was for "the time of the end" (verse 17), and so we are warned away from attempting to apply a literal translation of six years and four months from the time Rome came to power. There is more to it than that.

We can understand this vision about the sanctuary better when we review the religious services with which Daniel was familiar, which had been practiced in the Temple in Jerusalem before his exile. The Temple service was a continuation of that instituted by Moses in the wilderness when he built the first sanctuary, and that service is spelled out in detail in the books he wrote.

Each morning and evening an animal was sacrificed, reflecting the repentance of the people for their sins and recognizing that "the wages of sin is death" (Romans 6:23). The priest ate a portion of each sacrifice, thus symbolically partaking of the sins. In addition, the blood from the slain animals was sprinkled inside the sanctuary, in front of the veil that sealed off the place where the actual presence of God was manifest.

Once a year, on the Day of Atonement, a special animal was selected. No sins were placed upon its head. Yet it was slain and its blood taken right into the most sacred room. This "innocent" blood atoned for the year's accumulation of "sin-laden" blood, and the sanctuary was "cleansed," or set right. This yearly service was so important that any Israelite who did not participate in it was cut off from the people. And anyone who during the year had committed some sin for which they had not offered a sacrifice was cut off from the people. Thus the service was in essence a judgment, a time of accounting.

Here we see an important tie-in between the vision of chapter 8 and that of chapter 7. In the earlier vision Daniel was given a view of the judgment scene in heaven, with books of record opened and God Himself sitting on the throne. The little horn is judged guilty, and the kingdom is given to the Son of man and to His people. The earthly sanctuary was an illustration of what transpires in heaven; it was an object lesson of God's way of saving humanity. The writer of Hebrews describes the heavenly service in which Christ is both high priest and sacrifice. (See Hebrews 8 and 9.)

So the "two thousand and three hundred days" is a time element to be applied to the same situation as described in the first vision, namely, the judgment. That is why Gabriel told Daniel the vision was for "the time of the end."

The whole thing troubled the prophet; in fact, he says he fainted and was sick "certain days" (Daniel 8:27). Not only was he concerned for the integrity and honor of the Lord's name and worship; he was grieved to know that the period of desecration would be protracted.

The ninth chapter opens with Daniel still concerned for his Lord's honor. Several years have transpired since his second vision. As he studies the prophecies of Jeremiah, he reads that his people, the Jews, were to spend 70 years in Babylonian exile (Jeremiah 29:10). He ascertains that the time is near when they should be returning to Jerusalem. But there is that nagging memory of a vision wherein the sanctuary would be trodden underfoot, a vision that was to be "for many days" (Daniel 8:26). What did it mean? Was there to be a delay to the return? Were his people not to go back and rebuild the destroyed

Temple? Would God not honor His word? Or did the vision apply to something else?

Earnestly Daniel prayed that the Lord would fulfill His promise. On behalf of his people he confessed their waywardness, but he asked that the Lord be merciful. While he was praying, the angel Gabriel appeared to him again.

Right away we must determine the relationship between this appearance and the vision of chapter 8. In that earlier vision Gabriel had said, "Understand, O son of man: for at the time of the end shall be the vision" (verse 17). Yet Daniel did not understand. Although the ram and the goat were explained to him, he fainted before he had been given a clear explanation of the 2,300 days. He said, "I was astonished at the vision, but none understood it" (verse 27).

Now in the ninth chapter Daniel introduces Gabriel as the one "whom I had seen in the vision at the beginning" (verse 21), and Gabriel describes his purpose as "to give thee skill and understanding. . . . Therefore understand the matter, and consider the vision" (verses 22, 23). Obviously, it was the vision of chapter 8 that Daniel was to understand, and it was the time factor that yet remained to be explained.

"Seventy weeks are determined [or "cut off"] upon thy people and upon thy holy city, to finish the transgression, and to make an end of sins, and to make reconciliation for iniquity, and to bring in everlasting righteousness, and to seal up the vision and prophecy, and to anoint the most Holy" (verse 24).

A better translation has "weeks of years," instead of "weeks"; the angel was actually saying that 70 seven-year periods, or 490 years, would be allotted to Daniel's people, the Jews. They had had many opportunities to realize God's purpose for them, but they had spurned them all, going after the gods of the nations around them. God had delivered them into exile. But He would return them, and give them one more chance, 490 more years.

Gabriel went on to say that the period would begin with the "commandment to restore and to build Jerusalem" (verse 25). There were several such decrees, by Cyrus, by Darius, and by Artaxerxes. But the most effective one, the one that restored to the Jews their autonomy, took effect in 457 B.C. Sixty-nine weeks, the angel said, or 483 years, from that point would lead to the Messiah. And 483 years from 457 B.C., in A.D. 27, the fifteenth year of Tiberius Caesar, Jesus was baptized and anointed by the Holy Spirit (Messiah means "anointed").

One more seven-year period remained for the people of the covenant. "In the midst of the week he shall cause the sacrifice and the oblation to cease" (verse 27). Three and one-half years after His baptism, Jesus was crucified, putting an end to the system of sacrifices in the Temple. For a few more years the disciples of Jesus concentrated on preaching the gospel to the Jews. When the Jewish leaders killed the Christian deacon Stephen, the church scattered and began preaching to the Gentiles. The time allotted to the Jewish nation was complete, and never again would they hold special status in God's plan for humanity. Now "there is no difference between the Jew and the Greek" (Romans 10:12), and the words once spoken to the Hebrews, "Ye are a chosen generation, a royal priesthood, an holy nation, a peculiar people," are now applied to the Christian church. (Compare Exodus 19:5, 6 with 1 Peter 2:9.)

Some Bible students would take this seventieth week and separate it by more than 2,000 from the first

69. They say that it applies to a period yet future, after a supposed secret and invisible return of Christ; that it is a period when the Jews would again enjoy a special relationship with God. However, the New Testament clearly states that the Christian church now stands before God as Israel. It is also absurd that in a time prophecy one should be so cavalier in dealing with time. Why specify "seventy weeks," or 490 years, when there would be that much plus more than 2,000 years? Surely the seventieth week follows on the heels of the sixty-ninth week.

But back to the original vision. Gabriel told Daniel the 490-year period would be "cut off" (Daniel 9:26) and that it would not only witness the Advent of the Messiah but also "seal up the vision" (verse 24). When we relate this explanation of Gabriel's to the 2,300-day period of Daniel 8, the part Daniel did not at first understand, we conclude that the one is a part of the other. The 2,300 days represents so many years. This principle had been employed at least twice before in God's dealings with His people. (See Numbers 14:34 and Ezekiel 4:6.)

The 490-year period would be cut off from the 2,300-year period. The former would be for the Jews; the remainder would extend until the "sanctuary be cleansed." The baptism and crucifixion of Jesus and the gospel to the Gentiles occurred "when the fulness of time was come" (Galatians 4:4), which assures us that we are on the right track in regard to the starting date and method of calculation. Hence we can with confidence calculate that the remainder of the 2,300 years would extend to A.D. 1844. That was the time that the sanctuary was to be "cleansed" or "vindicated."

What sanctuary would be involved in any situation in 1844? Since the Mosaic sanctuary was gone, and its successor, the Temple at Jerusalem, had long been destroyed, the only sanctuary that could be meant in Daniel 8:14 would have to be the one in heaven, of which Christ is the minister, the high priest (Hebrews 8:1, 2).

As has been mentioned, the Aaronic priests daily mediated sins by means of the blood of sacrificed animals, and transferred the sins to the outer or first room of the sanctuary. Once a year, on the Day of Atonement, through a special service in the inner room, the sanctuary was "cleansed," or "justified." Parallel to this, yet with a contrast, Christ offered Himself in sacrifice for our sins only once. Until 1844 He conducted in heaven His mediatorial work analogous to the daily ministry of the Aaronic priests. From 1844 onward He has been involved in the inner-sanctuary work.

At that time Christ began making the personal application of the benefits of His sacrifice to individual sinners who had repented. At the same time, there began the work of examining the record books to see who had truly accepted Christ as their heavenly Mediator—in contrast to those who were depending on human mediators or on their own "goodness." Then also began the proclamation on earth of the work that was going on in heaven, calling attention to the heavenly mediatorial and judgmental process. This process would clear the record books, thus "cleansing" the heavenly sanctuary and vindicating the Christly priesthood that had been appropriated and abrogated by men on earth.

Thus the vision of Daniel 8 and 9 ends on the same triumphant note as the vision of Daniel 7 and the dream of Daniel 2. For a while the earthly kingdoms and powers may seem to triumph, but God is at work behind the scenes, and His purposes will prevail.

Meanwhile, the question of immediate concern to us is this: Is your name—and is mine—in Christ's book of life? Have we personally accepted Him as our mediator, our high priest? If so, then when He comes to our names in the holy record He will rejoice with the Father in our salvation, and we will celebrate our joy throughout eternity

In spite of the apparent dichotomy, the theme of the last half of the book of Daniel is the same as that of the first half—God will have His way in the affairs of earth. Christ and His followers will have full victory over all the forces of evil. Toward that end Christ takes a personal interest in each one of us.

A COSMIC CONFLICT

THE REMAINING three chapters of Daniel constitute one vision. Not surprisingly, this vision covers
the same ground as the earlier ones. Indeed, it has become apparent by now that the theme of the entire
book is to portray God's role in the sweep of history.
How fitting it is that Daniel, one of the highest-rank-
ing government officials in all the Bible, yet faithful
to God in any and all circumstances, should be the
one to reveal how God works behind the scenes to
bring about His will. And nowhere is this more
clearly brought to view than in the tenth chapter.

Again, Daniel has been concerned for his people.
Cyrus has issued a decree allowing the Jews to return
to their demolished Jerusalem and rebuild it, but things
haven't been going right. The Samaritans in the vicin-
ity have opposed the return of the exiles, and have
made representations to Cyrus that he reverse his
order. Would they prevail?

Daniel is in mourning and deep prayer for three
weeks. One day when he is out by the riverside he
looks up and sees "a certain man" (Daniel 10:5). In

comparing this Person's description with one given by John the revelator (Revelation 1:13-15), we can be certain that it was Jesus Himself whom Daniel saw. The prophet slumps to the ground, but an angel touches him, raises him up, and encourages him with the words that he is greatly beloved of Heaven. Then he explains why there has been a delay in answering Daniel's prayer.

"The prince of the kingdom of Persia withstood me one and twenty days" (Daniel 10:13), said the angel (who was probably Gabriel, the one who had conversed with Daniel on two different occasions). That was precisely the length of time Daniel had been in mourning. Indeed, the angel said that "from the first day that thou didst set thine heart to understand, and to chasten thyself before thy God, thy words were heard, and I am come for thy words" (verse 12).

To answer Daniel's prayer on behalf of his people had required a visit to Cyrus, king of Persia. But the powers of evil opposed the angel. The devil, the "prince of this world" (John 12:31), also fought for the king's will. Not until Michael, "one of the chief princes" (Daniel 10:13; the margin says "the first" prince), arrived on the scene was the victory obtained. "I remained there with the kings of Persia," the angel said. The original wording conveys the thought that "I alone remained," that is, the evil one was put to rout.

Who is this Michael, whose intervention was the decisive factor in the struggle for Cyrus' favor? The last verse of the chapter describes Him as "your prince," and Daniel 12:1 says He is "the great prince." He is mentioned again in Jude 9 as the "archangel." First Thessalonians 4:16 associates the voice of the archangel with the resurrection of the saints at the second coming of Jesus. In John 5:28, Jesus says it is His own voice that calls the dead from their graves. Adding "line upon line," then, we may identify Michael as Jesus Himself. And Jesus is the One whom Daniel saw by the river-side at the beginning of this vision.

Now we have the complete picture. Daniel is concerned that God's promise regarding the return of his people to their homeland might be thwarted by their enemies. Gabriel (for it must have been he) is sent immediately to answer Daniel's prayer. This means a visit to Cyrus, where he is opposed by Satan's emissaries. This reminds us of Paul's words: "For we are not contending against flesh and blood, but against the principalities, against the powers, against the world rulers of this present darkness, against the spiritual hosts of wickedness in the heavenly places" (Ephesians 6:12, RSV).

As reinforcement, Jesus Himself comes to aid Gabriel, and the adversary is put to rout. It is at this juncture that Jesus shows Himself to Daniel, and Gabriel explains what it is all about. Moreover, the angel reveals to Daniel, in the first verse of the next chapter, that he had worked with Darius, Cyrus's immediate predecessor, in a similar way, "to confirm and to strengthen him" (Daniel 11:1).

How wonderful it is to know that God takes a direct hand in our concerns! He doesn't force His will. Human beings are still allowed the power of choice. Every person ultimately decides his or her own destiny. God might have forced Cyrus to conform, but instead He pleaded with him for three weeks and fought off the evil one to keep him from imposing his will on the king. It may take a little longer this way, and in the meantime humanity may suffer, but human integrity remains intact, and God demonstrates that His method of government is infinitely superior to that of Satan.

What most people do not realize, and what this tenth chapter gives us a glimpse into, is that our daily affairs are not the only reality in the universe. There is a battle raging on a cosmic scale. We are not pawns but actual participants in that battle. Every decision we make in God's favor helps to vindicate Him in the great moral issues. And at last He will win. The outcome has already been decided, settled forever by the victory of Jesus at Calvary. What remains is the final disposition, and the question comes home to each of us, On whose side will we be? On the side of Him who made us and sets before us the way of life and salvation, or of him who has been so long in rebellion against the commandments of God?

In chapter 11 the angel outlines for Daniel the main part of the vision. An interesting aspect is immediately noticeable—the nations are no longer referred to by means of symbols. Daniel is an experienced prophet now; we too have had the benefit of the interpretations given to his earlier visions. So now the angel can speak plainly.

One by one the angel describes the kings that shall reign in Persia: after three kings (Cambyses, the False Smerdis, Darius I) there shall be a "far richer" king (Xerxes) who shall "stir up" Greece. With that latter power aroused and come to nationhood, a "mighty king shall stand up," Alexander the Great. But his kingdom will be broken and given to the "four winds of heaven." This division of Alexander's empire among his four generals was earlier depicted by an animal with four heads, and a goat with four horns.

Of these four powers (later reduced to three), the most important as far as the Jews were concerned were the Ptolemies of Egypt (the "king of the south") and the Seleucids of Asia Minor (the "king of the north") and their successors. With these parameters in mind, a student of history can readily trace the machinations of the Caesars and Cleopatra and other notables, all spelled out in the eleventh chapter of Daniel—hundreds of years before the events transpired!

And once again there is spread out for our consideration the relationship of pagan Rome toward the people of God, followed by the relationship of papal Rome toward the things of God: He "shall pollute the sanctuary of strength, and shall take away the daily sacrifice"; "he shall exalt himself, and magnify himself above every god, and shall speak marvellous things against the God of gods. . . . Neither shall he regard the God of his fathers, nor the desire of women" (Daniel 11:31, 36, 37). These are interpreted as referring to substitution of a human priesthood for the priesthood of Jesus Christ, who is the "one mediator between God and men" (1 Timothy 2:5); to the claim to forgive sins; and to the celibacy of priests.

Daniel 11:41 says this power "shall enter also into the glorious land," and verse 45 adds, "he shall plant the tabernacles of his palace between the seas in the glorious holy mountain." These references are interpreted as applying to Palestine, the Holy Land. Does prophecy envision a time when the Papacy will be a major influence in Jerusalem, perhaps even moving its seat of government there? Could current events involving Egypt, Israel, and other nations of the Mideast resolve into a fulfillment of these closing verses of Daniel 11? Perhaps it is too early to tell.

We do know that, as was pointed out concerning this same power at the close of the vision of Daniel 8, "he shall come to his end, and none shall help him" (Daniel 11:45). Grand alliances will be formed with various nations of the earth, and for a short time almost the whole world will be at his command. But it will not last, for God will have the final say.

"At that time," said the angel to Daniel, nearing the conclusion of his revelation, "shall Michael stand up, the great prince which standeth for the children of thy people: and there shall be a time of trouble, such as never was since there was a nation even to that same time: and at that time thy people shall be delivered, every one that shall be found written in the book" (Daniel 12:1). The angel identifies this time of trouble as just before the return of Christ, when the dead will be resurrected. "And many of them that sleep in the dust of the earth shall awake, some to everlasting life, and some to shame and everlasting contempt" (verse 2).

Daniel was ordered at this point to close up the book in which he was recording these visions: "But thou, O Daniel, shut up the words, and seal the book, even to the time of the end: many shall run to and fro, and knowledge shall be increased" (verse 4). This has been interpreted two ways: (1) when human knowledge would "explode," and travel would be multiplied across the face of the earth, and (2) when an understanding of prophecy itself, and of Daniel in particular, would blossom, and devout men and women would study as never before the things pertaining to the end of the age.

Either way, it is clear that the fulfillment of Daniel 12:4 is a reality. We are living in "the time of the end." In our time we may look for the closing events of each of these four great lines of prophecy. The "Son of man" is about to set up His kingdom, "which shall not be destroyed." It behooves us to take the necessary steps to assure citizenship in that kingdom.

Subsequent Bible writers, and Jesus Christ Himself, have done much to help us better understand the issues sketched in the book of Daniel. Jesus described the nature of His kingdom; He indicated that it consists of a present relationship between the individual soul and Him, as well as a very real and literal kingdom in which He in person will live and reign on earth, the visible and acknowledged ruler of all His saints.

Like Daniel, Jesus affirmed that the future is not to be judged by the present. God will have His way. While He was in bonds, being judged by a human tribunal, Jesus declared, "Hereafter shall ye see the Son of man sitting on the right hand of power, and coming in the clouds of heaven" (Matthew 26:64).

Paul also had much to say about the second coming of Jesus, when He would set up His kingdom. He spoke of the "judgment to come" (Acts 24:25), of the resurrection of the redeemed when "the Lord himself shall descend from heaven with a shout" (1 Thessalonians 4:16), and of when the impostor within the church would be revealed and destroyed (2 Thessalonians 2:8). Paul described the anticipation of the Lord's return as "that blessed hope" (Titus 2:13).

Is this great event a "blessed hope" to you? Are you looking forward to seeing Jesus in person? If He owns your heart, you are. If you are more attached to the things of this world, then you would dread Christ's coming as an interruption of your plans. Jesus is inviting, even pleading, with each person to accept Him as their great sin-bearer, mediator, king, and friend.

Daniel saw Him thus, and has left us with his book of prophecy that we might love God as he loved Him and that we might prepare for His kingdom.

But the best delineation of events surrounding the establishment of Christ's kingdom and of the cosmic warfare of which that establishment is the climax is provided by John in Revelation. It is to that book that we now turn our attention.

GOD'S
PERSONAL CONCERN
FOR HIS PEOPLE

WHEN JESUS told us to study and understand the book of Daniel, of course He did not tell us to study Revelation, because it had not yet been written. But He would have, had it been available, for it is a revelation of Himself. John, who wrote the book, included these words in the preamble: "Blessed is he that readeth, and they that hear the words of this prophecy, and keep those things which are written therein: for the time is at hand" (Revelation 1:3).

Even with this blessing, the book remains an enigma to many people. To be sure, there are parts of it the meaning of which no one can be absolutely certain (which is probably true to some degree of almost every book of the Bible). But some general principles of Bible study will do much to dispel the ambiguity.

The first principle to bear in mind is to read in context. Who was the author, to whom was he writing, and under what circumstances? What did he mean to say, in the setting of his day? John was a

Christian Jew writing to the Christian church as a whole. But his audience, by and large, considered themselves as Israel, the true Israel, the proper inheritors of the promises made to Abraham. They claimed this status on the basis of their faith in the One who had made the promises, even as Abraham had originally believed. Those who were Israel by the flesh only and who did not believe had lost claim to the inheritance (Matthew 21:43).

John wrote in apocalyptic style, a form of literature that had been fairly common within his culture for some hundreds of years. It took its distinctive features from the book of Daniel—writing centered upon last-day events; highly figurative language full of allegorical, surrealistic symbols; prose rather than the poetry that characterizes so much Hebrew literature; and concern for the cosmic, behind-the-scenes, over-reaching controversy between God and Satan that has this world as the battleground.

Because John wrote in an established style, some insight to his meaning may be gained from a familiarity with other literature in the same style, such as the book of Daniel. Similarly, a knowledge of history will help to clue the reader in to what John was writing about. He wrote at a time when pagan Rome was becoming ever more concerned about the inroads of the new religion, Christianity, and the challenge it posed to the state religion, emperor worship. (It was because of that concern that John himself was exiled to Patmos.) The message of the book had to be couched in such terms that Christians would understand, yet not get them into trouble with Roman authorities.

A second principle of prophetic interpretation is to read the message literally where possible. When a literal reading provides no meaning, we may look for a symbolic or figurative sense. A lamb that has seven horns and seven eyes certainly is a symbol. A slain lamb, and one who is the only being worthy of revealing the future, obviously represents Jesus Christ, "the Lamb of God, which taketh away the sin of the world" (John 1:29).

A third principle is to let the Bible explain itself. We have noted, for instance, the relationship between Daniel and Revelation. In the former book a beast represents a political power; multiple heads denote subdivisions of that power, and horns and crowns emphasize the political nature. Other Bible writers used symbols also, and we can borrow from these when interpreting Revelation. Hosea and Paul used the figure of a woman, a bride, as a symbol of the church. Ezekiel used a time symbol—one day in prophecy, particularly apocalyptic prophecy, often represents a year of literal time. The interpretations of Daniel made use of this terminology, and we shall meet it again in the book of Revelation.

John left no ambiguity as to the purpose and thrust of his message—it was to reveal Jesus Christ, to show "things which must shortly come to pass" (Revelation 1:1). "Behold, he cometh with clouds," John declared, "and every eye shall see him" (verse 7). Here in a nutshell is what the book is all about.

Like the visions of Daniel, Revelation may be organized into four great lines of prophecy: the letters to the seven churches (chapters 1-3), the events that transpired under the seven seals (chapters 4-7), the tragedies of the seven trumpets (chapters 8-11), and the final events, the wrap-up of history (chapters 12-22). This is a generalization, however, for there are elements of final events included in the first three sections.

Also, the visions of Revelation are not identified as

to where one vision closes and another begins. Indeed, it is possible that it was all revealed at one time, but that probably would have been too much for the elderly man to bear or remember.

John was on Patmos as an exile for his faith. History and archaeology attest to a penal colony on that small island in the Aegean Sea. The prophet doesn't mention it, but he may have done slave labor in a rock quarry there. One Sabbath day he saw a familiar figure. It was the "Son of man," his own beloved Lord, Jesus Christ. John had known Him as a humble teacher, an ex-carpenter. But following His ascension, Jesus had been elevated to the glory He had known before His sojourn on earth. John saw Him clothed in regal garments, with a belt of gold. His eyes were as flames of fire, and "out of his mouth went a sharp twoedged sword" (verse 16). His overall appearance was as the dazzling sun.

John realized he was in vision; there were elements in what he saw, such as the great sword, that were intended to convey a message of power and glory, of conquest and strength. John fell as though dead, but Jesus lifted him up and commissioned him to write what he saw, for the benefit of the churches. And so we have the privilege of seeing, through John's eyes, "the things which shall be hereafter" (verse 19). John saw these things while in the power of the Holy Spirit. We should pray that the same Spirit will help us to understand.

Jesus was standing amid seven golden candlesticks, and He held in His hands seven stars. He told John the seven candlesticks were "the seven churches," and the stars were the angels of the churches. John was to transcribe a message for each church. Thus Jesus indicated His concern for His people. Although He cannot be with us personally, through His Spirit He will be with us "alway," He said, "even unto the end of the world" (Matthew 28:20).

The seven churches named in chapters 2 and 3 were companies of believers in actual towns on the mainland not far from John's post of exile. They were churches that he had probably visited and cared for. Christ was concerned for them. One by one, all the apostles but John had passed from the scene, and he had not many more years. But Jesus would continue still as their God and their protector.

But these seven messages were not to be limited to seven geographical locations. Jesus had said, "to the churches." There were many more than these seven. So they were all to share in the messages. And not only the churches then in existence but others that would follow, on down to our own day. All who make up the church of Jesus on earth may find a message for themselves in these two chapters.

Jesus spoke words of commendation and encouragement. He also gave warnings and dire threatenings. It was all done in love. These messages have been interpreted by the church down through the centuries as applying to various phases or periods that the church has passed through. They may also represent certain types of situations that any given church, or an individual believer, may experience. Their message is universal.

The church at Ephesus, for instance, was commended for its patience, but Jesus was disappointed in that it had lost its "first love." This, then, could represent the early believers, the "apostolic church." But it could also speak of a person whose fervor and devotion, experienced at conversion, has waned. Jesus told a parable about a sower who went forth to sow.

Some of his seed fell on stony ground. It took root, but when the sun grew hot it withered and died. Jesus said that would happen to a person who let the cares of this world crowd out the love of God.

But He extends a wonderful promise: "To him that overcometh will I give to eat of the tree of life, which is in the midst of the paradise of God" (Revelation 2:7).

The church members at Smyrna suffered. Many were cast into prison; others were killed. In addition, they experienced turncoats among them, and deceivers. "Ye shall have tribulation ten days," Jesus said (verse 10). This could be a prophecy of the 10 years of especially severe persecution that the Christians suffered under Diocletian and his successors, from A.D. 303 to 313. But Paul said that "all that will live godly in Christ Jesus shall suffer persecution" (2 Timothy 3:12). There are many people who are in prison today because of their faith. Others have lost their jobs because they cannot in conscience work on the day God has set apart as holy. Still others suffer the ostracism of their friends, or even have been disowned by their families. The promise to the church at Smyrna applies to all such: "He that overcometh shall not be hurt of the second death" (Revelation 2:11).

The churches in Pergamos and Thyatira had many commendable qualities. In Pergamos they held fast Christ's name in spite of satanic elements in their midst. This church well represents the period when worldly influences pressed upon the people of God, causing many to apostatize. They kept the name of Christian but adopted the practices and philosophies of the pagans. It was during this period that the first day of the week, Sunday, devoted to sun worship, gradually replaced God's Sabbath, the seventh day of the week.

The Sabbath-Sunday question will again become a major focus in the great cosmic conflict, pitting as it does the created against the Creator. Jesus' warning to the church of Pergamos, and to all who lose the distinction between God's commandments and those that are merely human, is: "Repent; or else I will come unto thee quickly, and will fight against them with the sword of my mouth" (verse 16). "In vain they do worship me," Jesus had said, "teaching for doctrines the commandments of men" (Matthew 15:9).

Thyatira was commended for its works, and for charity, service, faith, and patience. However, Jesus perceived a tendency to give ear to seducing doctrines, represented in the prophecy by the figure of Jezebel, the wicked wife of King Ahab. She had introduced idol worship into Israel in the days of Elijah. The message to Thyatira, and to all the Christian church, is that God can accept only pure allegiance. There must be no spiritual "adultery," no dallying with the allurements of the world.

Most of the church members at Sardis, it seems, were spiritual zombies. "Thou hast a name that thou livest, and art dead" (Revelation 3:1). Their names were on the church records, but they did not live the life of Christ. Only a few had kept themselves undefiled by worldly influences. Yet the promise is made, "He that overcometh, the same shall be clothed in white raiment; and I will not blot out his name out of the book of life, but I will confess his name before my Father, and before his angels" (verse 5).

Philadelphia was the sixth church. The name means "brotherly love." The members were commended because they had kept Christ's word and had not denied Him. A special message is given to this church: "These things saith he that is holy, he that is true, he that hath the key of David, he that openeth, and no man shutteth; and shutteth, and no man openeth . . . : behold, I have set before thee an open door, and no man can shut it" (verses 7, 8).

In the historical interpretation of these seven letters to the churches, Philadelphia would apply to that time when the 2300-day prophecy of Daniel 8 and 9 met its fulfillment. It will be recalled that this prophetic period began in 457 B.C., when Artaxerxes issued his decree that Jerusalem might be restored and enjoy autonomy. Seventy weeks, or 490 years, extended to the time of Jesus, and the entire period ended in A.D. 1844. This was when the heavenly sanctuary was to be "cleansed," or set right, in the great investigative judgment. This work would proceed first with those who had died, and then pass on to the living.

The judgment process, evaluating as it does the claims of people to the mercy of God, determines whether they may indeed receive that mercy. Have they been faithful to God? If in the judgment it has been found that they have been faithful, then the door to eternal life is open to them. But if it is found that theirs is an empty profession, that they have denied their Lord, then the door is forever closed.

The message to Philadelphia, although applying particularly to those living at about 1844, still applies today, for the sanctuary work then begun in heaven is still in progress. You and I may join in the blessings promised to the Philadelphians.

The last of the seven messages is to the church at Laodicea. This is described as a lukewarm church, "neither cold nor hot" (verse 15). Its members think they need nothing, but they are naked and miserable. They trust in their own righteousness; they need to recognize their need for the righteousness of Christ. But God has not forsaken them by any means. "As many as I love, I rebuke and chasten: be zealous therefore, and repent" (verse 19). God's threats and warnings are given in love. They are made to direct us to Him.

Notice the individual appeal that is implicit in each of the messages: "To him that overcometh . . ." The messages are directed to the church, but also to each person. This is particularly evident in the seventh message: "Behold, I stand at the door, and knock" (verse 20). This refers to the heart door, where each person makes the decision as to what will have a part in their life and what will rule there. God does not force His way in; we have the choice to admit Him or refuse Him.

If we let Jesus enter our hearts, He will let us enter His Father's house. If we let Him share our lives, He will share with us the joys of eternal life. If we yield to Him the throne of our hearts, He will share with us the throne of His Father's kingdom.

Note how closely the conclusion to each of these letters ties in with the climaxing scenes of Daniel's visions. Jesus is directing the attention of the church to the coming day of victory. You and I may suffer now, but if we are faithful, we will triumph with Him at last.

SEVEN SEALS AND
SEVEN TRUMPETS

THE FAITHFUL apostle John was afforded a scene that is highly reminiscent of the one Daniel was given in his first vision. John looked into the throne room in heaven. He saw the divine Ruler of the universe sitting on the throne. Awesomely the prophet described Him, being careful not to seem to be limiting Him with merely human terms.

In his vision John saw 24 lesser thrones surrounding the throne of God. Those who sat on them were called "elders," and are identified as human beings who had lived on earth, for they praised Jesus for having redeemed them by His blood "out of every kindred, and tongue, and people, and nation" (Revelation 5:9). These may have included Enoch and Elijah and Moses, who the Bible specifically tells us were taken to heaven, the first two even without dying. The others of the 24 may have been resurrected in a special resurrection when Christ arose from the grave (Matthew 27:52, 53).

John describes four more creatures who make up God's court. The descriptions used—"like a lion," "like a calf," "like a flying eagle," "a face as a man"—seem to indicate that these living creatures are intended to teach us something symbolic about the nature of God and His government. They may connote, for example, God's sovereignty, His strength, His intelligence, His kingship. In addition to these creatures, there was the innumerable company of angels that Daniel had seen, "ten thousand times ten thousand, and thousands of thousands" (Revelation 5:11).

While this vast throng of heavenly beings was acclaiming the honor and power of Him who sat on the throne, that august Person produced a "book," no doubt a scroll, that was sealed with seven seals. It was the custom in John's day for important documents, such as a will, to be thus sealed. Only the person with the proper authority could open the seals with impunity. In his vision John saw the heavenly host deeply agitated, for there was apparently no one qualified to open the book God held. John also joined in the grieving.

Then his attention focused on a Lamb "as it had been slain" that had seven horns and seven eyes (verse 6). Throughout Bible times the number seven denoted perfectness or wholeness. This Lamb was further described as being the Lion of Judah, the Root of David. These were Messianic terms, just as a lamb was a Messianic figure. John was seeing a representation of Jesus Christ, who is perfect or complete in power, in wisdom, and in the Spirit.

The Lamb came forward and took the book. Immediately all those who had been so intently watching broke out into rapturous songs of praise: "Worthy is the Lamb that was slain to receive power, and riches, and wisdom, and strength, and honour, and glory, and blessing" (verse 12).

John watched closely as Jesus, the Lamb of God, took the book and opened the seals one by one. As He did so, John was treated to a preview of "things which must be hereafter" (Revelation 4:1). Upon the opening of the first seal John saw a splendid white horse, with a rider who wore a crown and carried a bow; he "went forth conquering" (Revelation 6:2).

In quick succession as each seal was opened John saw, after the white horse, a red horse, and authority was given to its rider "to take peace from the earth"; then there followed a black horse, whose rider carried a pair of balances in his hand; next a pale horse, whose rider was labeled Death, "and Hell followed with him" (verses 4–8).

In the fifth seal John was introduced to the subject of those who lost their lives because of their faith. Martyrs to the cause of God, their situation called for justice. John, most of whose fellow apostles had given their lives in testimony to their faith, and who himself was in exile for the same reason, empathized with these martyrs. But the time of their vindication had not yet arrived.

With the opening of the sixth seal we are on more familiar ground as far as symbolic imagery is concerned, and it gives us a perspective in which to place the five earlier seals. Here John witnessed a great earthquake; the sun became "black as sackcloth of hair, and the moon became as blood" (Revelation 7:12). Nor was that all. The stars fell, the heavens broke up, and the mountains and islands were shifted out of place.

This is familiar because Jesus had warned of such phenomena. "Immediately after the tribulation of those days," He said to His disciples on Mount Olivet, "shall the sun be darkened, and the moon shall not give her light, and the stars shall fall from heaven, and the powers of the heavens shall be shaken" (Matthew 24:29). These events were to precede closely His return from heaven: "And then shall appear the sign of the Son of man in heaven: and then shall all the tribes of the earth mourn, and they shall see the Son of man coming in the clouds of heaven with power and great glory" (verse 30).

In his vision John also saw that "the kings of the earth, and the great men, and the rich men" and many others "hid themselves in the dens and in the rocks of the mountains; and said to the mountains and rocks, Fall on us, and hide us from the face of him that sitteth on the throne, and from the wrath of the Lamb" (Revelation 6:15, 16).

This sixth seal, then, refers to the climax of earth's history, when Jesus prepares to return to earth, this time not as a baby or as a carpenter, but as Lord of all. Those of earth who are considered great by human standards but who have ignored the God of heaven will mourn their fate. Instinctively they will realize at last whom they have been fighting.

We can see now that the first five seals refer to situations that prevail between the time of John and the second coming of Jesus. At first, after Jesus left this earth, the church of God was pure and noble, like a white horse. Then in progressive stages apostasy crept in; the horse changed in color from red to black and then to the paleness of death. There was a long period when the official church, ostensibly the body of Christ, actually put to death those who were truly following the Lord's commandments. Millions of faithful believers were burned, hanged, quartered, flung from cliffs, killed in various ways, because they did not conform to the state-supported religion. Just as

71

the blood of Abel, killed by his brother, Cain, cried to the Lord for vengeance (Genesis 4:10), so these deaths demanded justice. And that time of justice would come, as we noted in studying Daniel 7 and as we will further see in the book of Revelation.

Although Revelation 6:15 says that "every bond-man, and every free man" hid from the wrath of the Lamb, and although Jesus said that "then shall all the tribes of the earth mourn" (Matthew 24:30), there will be a few who will rejoice in His appearing. "The great day of his wrath is come; and who shall be able to stand?" (Revelation 6:17) ask the ones who hide; the answer comes in the next few verses: "the servants of our God," who bear His seal in their foreheads (Revelation 7:3).

There follows a remarkable description of those who will be delivered from the cataclysmic events that surround the return of Jesus. It is a special group of 144,000 people, 12,000 from each of the tribes of "Israel." Bear in mind that it is the Israel of the gospel that is here spoken of, not national Israel. When the nation rejected Jesus and the kingdom of salvation that He offered, the covenant made with Abraham was withdrawn from national Israel and extended to those who have been baptized in Christ (Galatians 3:29). Therefore, all who honor Christ are "Israel" in the New Testament sense (see Galatians 6:16).

Whether or not this 144,000 is a literal figure, it certainly doesn't represent all who will be saved in the kingdom of God. John says, "I beheld, and, lo, a great multitude, which no man could number, of all nations, and kindreds, and people, and tongues, stood before the throne, and before the Lamb, clothed with white robes, and palms in their hands" (Revelation 7:9). This throng, all the redeemed of earth from

Abel's time forward, praise God for their salvation. They heap upon Him "blessing, and glory, and wisdom, and thanksgiving, and honour, and power, and might" (verse 12). What a tribute that will be!

Only one short sentence describes the contents of the seventh seal: "There was silence in heaven about the space of half an hour" (Revelation 8:1). That is all that is said. Perhaps it applies to the destruction of the wicked, those who had aligned themselves with the evil one, those who called for the mountains to fall on them. Some of these will have relatives, even loved ones, among the number who are saved. Indeed, some no doubt will have considered themselves as on the side of God, but little by little they have alienated themselves from His true will. From God's viewpoint, who is "not willing that any should perish, but that all should come to repentance" (2 Peter 3:9), this time of reckoning may be a sad period, even for the unfallen angels.

Then again, this "half an hour" of silence in heaven may represent, in prophetic timekeeping, the period when heaven is emptied of angels, for they have all come to earth with Christ, who claims His kingdom. One way or another, it marks a great occasion in the controversy between God and Satan.

But right away John goes into another line of prophecy. He sees seven angels, each with a trumpet, and as each angel blows, tremendous events take place. At the first blowing, "hail and fire mingled with blood" (Revelation 8:7) rain upon the earth, and a third part of the trees of earth are burned up. At the second sounding, a burning mountain falls into the sea, a third part of the sea turns to blood, and a third of the navies of earth are destroyed. At the blowing of the fourth trumpet, a third part of the sun, moon, and stars are darkened.

Bad as the first four trumpets were, the remaining

three are even more terrible. The imagery is almost too complicated to paraphrase here. Smoke comes out of a bottomless pit; the smoke turns out to be locusts, but the locusts have the shape of horses, with faces like men's faces, hair like women's hair, and teeth like lion's teeth. They had power "to hurt men five months" (Revelation 9:10).

Under the sixth trumpet, "the four angels which are bound in the great river Euphrates" were loosed "for an hour, and a day, and a month, and year" to slay a third of the men on earth (verses 14, 15). John saw a great army of horsemen, "two hundred thousand thousand" (200 million). Fire, smoke, and brimstone came out of the horses' mouths (verse 17).

Through the centuries the church has believed these trumpets to correspond to political events that have some bearing upon the people of God. Beginning in John's time, they would refer to the persecution perpetrated first by pagan Rome on the Christians, then by papal Rome on nonconformists. Then there was the devastation wreaked by followers of the prophet Mohammed as they extended their influence over much of Europe.

An interesting confirmation, both of the concept of the trumpets as a whole and of the principle of prophetic interpretation whereby a day in prophecy represents a year of literal time, was accomplished in the nineteenth century. According to that principle, the time periods of Revelation 9:5 and 9:15 represent 541 years and 15 days. A Bible student named Josiah Litch believed, as others had before him as far back as Martin Luther, that the Ottoman Empire was the power referred to under the sixth trumpet. Based on the date that the Ottomans got the upper hand over the Byzantine Empire, in A.D. 1299, Litch concluded that the Ottomans would come to the end of their power in August 1840. Later he settled on August 11 as the exact date. As events transpired, that was the very date that the Ottoman sultan acquiesed to an arrangement whereby the powers of Britain, Austria, Prussia, and Russia decided affairs of state for him.

But there is one more trumpet to go. Revelation 11:15 says, "The seventh angel sounded; and there were great voices in heaven, saying, The kingdoms of this world are become the kingdoms of our Lord, and of his Christ; and he shall reign for ever and ever." There you have it. The final event in the political history of this world, the history of the nations, is when Jesus establishes His nation. It shall supersede and encompass all others. Truly He will be "King of kings and Lord of lords." Through all the play and counterplay on earth, God is working out His will, sometimes quietly, sometimes with dramatic effect. Humans may think they are running things their way, but at last the true Ruler will be revealed. That is the theme of the book of Daniel, that is the theme running throughout Revelation, and that is the theme of this book. God has a grand design, and unfolding history will reveal it. We are on the edge of God's forever.

The remainder of the book of Revelation shows how all this will come about.

THE ENEMY OF
THE CHURCH

RIGHT IN the heart of the book of Revelation (the twelfth chapter) is a passage that portrays, better than any other in the entire Bible, the great cosmic controversy between God, particularly Christ, and Satan. Although symbols are used here also, they are so transparent that there can be no doubt as to their meaning. Indeed, one chief protagonist is identified in just so many words.

John sees a majestic woman, "clothed with the sun, and the moon under her feet, and upon her head a crown of twelve stars" (Revelation 12:1). Again and again throughout the Bible a woman is used as a figure of the people of God. "I have likened the daughter of Zion [Israel] to a comely and delicate woman," says Jeremiah (Jeremiah 6:2). Paul wrote of the church, "I have espoused you to one husband, that I may present you as a chaste virgin to Christ" (2 Corinthians 11:2). In Revelation 12, then, the woman represents the church of God on earth.

The woman is opposed by a dragon, clearly identified as the devil, Satan. He had at one time been in heaven but, as John says, he was cast out. Jesus told of witnessing this event (Luke 10:18). Ezekiel 28 describes how Satan (presented under the figure of the king of Tyre) had at one time been an honored angel with a position near the throne of God. But somehow pride took root in his heart, and he magnified himself against God. The Ruler of the universe could have destroyed him right away, but he had presented himself so cunningly and deceptively to the other angels that these would not have understood God's actions. So God allowed Satan to develop his principles, even though they were based on deceit and selfishness, the very opposite of God's character.

Satan was expelled from heaven, however; he could not be allowed to remain there. "He was cast out into the earth, and his angels [the ones who were deceived by him and took his side] were cast out with him" (Revelation 12:9). According to the fourth verse of Revelation 12, these amounted to about a third of all the angels of heaven—a formidable army indeed. Nevertheless, God's power is greater; just two of God's angels overcame all the host of evil ones that tried to keep Jesus in the tomb.

But back to the drama that John witnessed. The woman gave birth to a male child, Jesus Himself. After Jesus ascended to heaven, the devil sought to destroy the woman, the church. She fled into the wilderness, where she was sheltered for "a thousand two hundred and threescore days" (verse 6). This 1,260-day period matches exactly with the time that the "little horn" of Daniel 7:25 would prevail. In fact, in Revelation 12:14 is found the same expression of time that Daniel used. It is the period of papal supremacy, when those who conscientiously put God's will first were persecuted by the power that had the name of the church but used the tactics of the dragon.

When the dragon or serpent or devil, or Satan, brought about a "flood" of persecution to destroy the woman, the earth itself swallowed the flood. Just about the time that the 1,260-year period expired (A.D. 1798), great new lands across the seas were opened as places of refuge for those who could not acquiesce to state-controlled religions. North America was one of these lands, where religious liberty took root and flourished.

The devil was temporarily thwarted, but by no means rendered impotent. "The dragon was wroth with the woman, and went to make war with the remnant of her seed, which keep the commandments of God, and have the testimony of Jesus Christ" (verse 17). Here is clearly identified the opponents and the issues of the controversy. The devil is angry at the church—the true church, those who make up the real body of Christ on earth. These are identified as those who keep the commandments of God and have the testimony of Jesus.

Many so-called Christian bodies claim that the law of God was abrogated by the death of Christ, but Christ Himself said, "Think not that I am come to destroy the law, or the prophets: I am not come to destroy, but to fulfil" (Matthew 5:17). And many Christian bodies say that one commandment of the 10 is no longer binding. But James says, "Whosoever shall keep the whole law, and yet offend in one point, he is guilty of all" (James 2:10).

But this true church in the last days, the "remnant" of the "seed" of the woman, is not legalistic in its faith. Its members do not expect salvation simply because they keep the commandments. They have "the testimony of Jesus." Jesus alone is the source of their salvation, and they keep His commandments out of love for Him, as an expression of their faith.

Then John witnesses a detailed presentation of just how Satan expects to prevail over the church. He sees a creature rise up out of the sea. It has seven heads and 10 horns, and on each horn is a crown. Across the heads are the names of blasphemy. John further describes this animal as having the body of a leopard, the feet of a bear, and the mouth of a lion. The creature received "power and authority" from the dragon, Satan.

Immediately we see that this beast has all the elements of the four beasts of Daniel's first vision, including the "little horn" that came up out of the fourth beast. It even has "a mouth speaking great things and blasphemies" (Revelation 13:5). Moreover, power is given to it for 42 months—1,260 days, or 1,260 literal years—just like the "little horn."

The clear conclusion is that Satan used in turn each of the nations that were outlined in Daniel's visions—Babylon, Medo-Persia, Greece, Rome. It is also clear that papal Rome may rightly be considered an extension of pagan Rome. The fact that the beast in John's vision had seven heads, not just the five powers referred to in Daniel 7, would indicate that it goes back to include Egypt and Assyria. Each of these powers in turn warred against the people of God.

John saw another beast, this one coming up out of the earth. It had lamblike horns but spoke like a dragon. It worked great wonders, exercising the same power and practicing the same evil work as the first beast. Indeed, it made an image to the first beast and forced everyone to worship it.

The first beast suffered a "deadly wound" to one of its seven heads, a wound that later healed.

This relates to that blow given to the Papacy when in 1798 General Berthier put Pope Pius VI under arrest and took him into exile. Seventy years later the Papacy had another setback when the Papal States were taken from it. Not until 1929 were the civil powers it once enjoyed returned.

It was about the time of this "deadly wound" that the second beast appeared, and that adds one more clue to its identity. As a beast it represents a civil power; coming up out of the earth (as opposed to rising from the sea, as did the first beast) would signify that this second beast arose in a sparsely populated part of earth ("sea" in vision is a symbol for many people—see Revelation 17:15); and the time of its appearance would be about A.D. 1798. With these identifying features, our attention is focused on the United States.

According to the prophecy, this power would be lamblike in some respects, but the time would come when it would speak "as a dragon" and make an image to the first beast. It would produce a program of religion-by-force similar to that for which the first power was notorious. It would cause all, "both small and great, rich and poor, free and bond, to receive a mark in their right hand, or in their foreheads: and that no man might buy or sell, save he that had the mark, or the name of the beast, or the number of his name" (Revelation 13:16, 17).

Some of the aspects of this prophecy have already been fulfilled. The days of ancient Babylon and the other kingdoms have come and gone. We are now in the days of the seventh "head," the Papacy. It has received its "deadly wound," and that is now well-nigh healed. The second beast has appeared, and at any time could start building an image to the first beast by restricting religious freedom, perhaps as an answer to an energy crisis or an economic setback or other catastrophe. There yet remains the setting of a "mark" and the death decree on all who refuse it.

What is this "mark of the beast"? The answer is not given in this chapter, but our minds go back to the seventh chapter of Revelation, where God sets His seal on His people. That seal is defined in Scripture; surely the "mark" of the beast, the great power that opposes God, would be a counterfeit of, or at least an opposing insignia counter to, God's seal.

Then what is the seal of God? An official seal is an insignia of authority. It comprises several parts: it names the authority and delineates the responsibility. A clear clue as to what is God's seal is given by the prophet Ezekiel, a man of God who served almost contemporaneously with Daniel. In Ezekiel 20:20 we read, "Hallow my Sabbaths; and they shall be a sign between me and you, that ye may know that I am the Lord your God."

The Ten Commandments are God's official law. He spoke it personally to Israel, and then He wrote it with His own finger on stone tablets. In the heart of those Ten Commandments we find His seal—the insignia of His authority and power. The fourth commandment closes with these words: "For in six days the Lord made heaven and earth, the sea, and all that in them is, and rested the seventh day: wherefore the Lord blessed the sabbath day, and hallowed it" (Exodus 20:11).

The Sabbath commandment is the only one that spells out which God ordered the commandments— it is the Creator God, the one who made and owns all the universe. Here is His seal on the law, and He says this is a sign of allegiance to Him. Conceivably, from a legal standpoint, a person could keep all the other nine commandments and not even claim to be a God-fearing person. But the proper observance of this commandment marks one as concerned for the honor and glory of the Creator.

The adversary of God, in his attempt to set up an opposing government, has produced his counterfeit to the seal of God in the form of Sunday as a day of worship. The seventh-day Sabbath was established by God in Eden as a memorial to His creative power, and hence its observance would be an acknowledgment of His right to the worship and allegiance of all created beings. On the other hand, the first day of the week has been used since ancient times to honor the sun. Paul announced that "the wrath of God is revealed from heaven against all ungodliness and unrighteousness of men, who hold the truth in unrighteousness" (Romans 1:18). These "changed the truth of God into a lie, and worshipped and served the creature more than the Creator, who is blessed for ever" (verse 25).

When he was yet in heaven, an angel before the presence of God, Satan's name was Lucifer, which means "day star" (Isaiah 14:12). Thus, in getting men to worship the sun, or to keep holy the first day of the week, which had so long been dedicated to the sun, Satan has in reality been successful in getting humanity to worship him. That the church, many, many years after Christ, should confer sanctity on this day by no means changes God's position.

Thus the Sabbath versus Sunday controversy is actually the focus, the pivotal point, of the cosmic controversy between God and Satan. It is more than just a matter of two different days; it is a matter of to whom we give allegiance!

As one more item of identification of the power under consideration in Revelation 13, the prophet adds this note: "Here is wisdom. Let him that hath understanding count the number of the beast: for it is the number of a man; and his number is Six hundred threescore and six" (verse 18).

The identification already supplied concerning this beast is sufficient to confirm that it does indeed represent the Papacy. Now we are directed to look for a name. It is to be the name or title of a man and, according to the first verse, one that usurps a divine prerogative. Since Reformation times a name fitting this description has been identified as one of the titles of the pope, VICARIVS FILII DEI, "Vicar of the Son of God." The numerical value of this name (V = 5, I = 1, C = 100, L = 50, D = 500) is 666.

When Jesus was describing to His disciples His second coming and the signs that would precede it, He said, "There shall arise false Christs" (Matthew 24:24). During Paul's ministry there were those who expected Christ to return at any moment. But he reminded them that "that day shall not come, except there come a falling away first, and that man of sin be revealed, the son of perdition; who opposeth and exalteth himself above all that is called God, or that is worshipped; so that he as God sitteth in the temple of God, shewing himself that he is God" (2 Thessalonians 2:3, 4).

This describes the power we have been studying in Revelation 13. The papal head claims, in effect, many of the prerogatives of the Godhead. He claims to be the vicar of the Son of God, to have the power to forgive sin, to cast down angels from heaven, and even to create nothing less than the actual body of Christ; and he claims infallibility in proclaiming matters of doctrine and morals.

Revelation 13:6 notes that this power sets itself in opposition to God's tabernacle, and them that dwell in heaven. In setting up a human priesthood, the papal system maligns the tabernacle service of God, for only Jesus Christ is high priest, the "one mediator between God and men" (1 Timothy 2:5).

Moreover, the claim that each time Mass is consecrated the priest is actually creating the body of Christ belittles the sacrifice of Jesus Christ on Calvary. The author of Hebrews goes to great length to make the point that Jesus offered Himself only once: "This man, after he had offered one sacrifice for sins for ever, sat down on the right hand of God; from henceforth expecting till his enemies be made his footstool. For by one offering he hath perfected for ever them that are sanctified" (Hebrews 10:12-14).

John said that the spirit that was to characterize antichrist was abroad in the world even in his day (1 John 4:3). The attitude of putting self first, of denying the efficacy of the gospel of Christ, of depending on human effort, of coercing religious allegiance—all this is basic to the spirit of antichrist.

After noting the characteristics and work of the antichrist in Revelation 13, John's attention is turned to the other side of the great controversy. On Mount Sion, or Zion, the traditional name for the seat of God's government, are 144,000 people. They have the heavenly Father's name written on their foreheads, and are obviously the same as are mentioned in the seventh chapter as having received the seal of God.

This scene is in heaven, not in earthly Jerusalem, for the throng sing "a new song" (Revelation 14:3) before the throne of God and before the 24 elders and the four living creatures, all of whom are described in the fourth chapter as being inside heaven itself. The

144,000 have been redeemed by the sacrifice of Jesus Christ, the Lamb of God, and the song they sing is one that only those who know what it is like to have been redeemed from sin can appreciate.

> "Holy, holy, is what the angels sing,
>   And I expect to help them make the courts of heaven ring;
> But when I sing redemption's story, they will fold their wings,
>   For angels never felt the joys that our salvation brings."
>
> —Johnson Oatman, Jr.

Of these 144,000, it is said that they are not defiled, and no guile or deceit was found in them. That is not to say that they have never sinned, but rather that Jesus has completely forgiven them and cleansed them of sin. They are "redeemed," bought by the very life of Jesus Himself. The group, then, is not exclusive. You and I could be in that number. Their victory is obtained, not through their merits, but through Jesus Christ. And He is available to us all.

GOD'S LAST WARNING

JOHN'S REVELATION is full of surprising turns and dramatic vistas. One scene seems to crowd in on another, showing various locales and representing different time periods. Sometimes there is an immediate relationship between adjoining scenes, and sometimes the relationship is distant or indistinct. Often the chronology is uncoordinated. Careful study is required to unravel the skeins, and in some cases we can't be sure of the final answer. The main message is that God will finally triumph; of that we can be certain.

In Revelation 14:6 John says, "I saw another angel fly in the midst of heaven." He had seen many angels, and certain ones had spoken to him directly, but this flying angel was the first of a series of three, as we notice in the ninth verse.

This angel has the "everlasting gospel to preach unto them that dwell on the earth, and to every nation, and kindred, and tongue, and people." The gospel of salvation in Jesus Christ is the everlasting gospel. It is always the same. Jesus Himself never changes (Hebrews 13:8), His law does not change, and His gospel does not change. His way of saving people who are guilty of breaking the law has ever been the same. Abraham was saved by faith. He saw that the sacrifices he offered were only a type of when God would provide Himself a sacrifice (Genesis 22:8).

There are those who speak of "dispensations." They teach that God deals in different ways with humankind in different eras, an arbitrary differentiation in His plan of salvation. It is from this basis that the idea of a secret rapture of the church arises. The doctrine is based on the idea that God has a different plan for national Israel than He has for the church. According to this theory, the time will come when Jesus will secretly remove the church from the world—Christians will disappear and go to heaven—and then God will revert back to an earlier plan for national Israel. After seven years He will return, this time visibly, and set up a throne in Jerusalem.

But we have already seen that God no longer has special plans for national Israel. Jesus told them that the kingdom of God would be taken from them and given to "a nation bringing forth the fruits thereof" (Matthew 21:43). Peter identified that successor nation as the church (1 Peter 2:9). The promises made to national Israel were only conditional—and they had not lived up to the conditions (see Jeremiah 18:1-10).

As for the seven years that the rapture theory interposes between a supposed secret coming of Christ (there is no place in all Scripture that indicates such a secret coming), they are based on the seventieth week, or seven-year period, of Daniel 9:24-27. But, as noted in that study, it is unrealistic to suppose a 2,000-year gap (between Christ's time and ours) in a time period of only 490 years.

And now we see that God does not deal in dispensations anyway: He does not have a different way of saving Jews than He has for saving anyone else. The gospel is an "everlasting gospel," and it is for every nation, kindred, tongue, and people.

Notice what this first angel of Revelation 14 proclaims: "Fear God, and give glory to him; for the hour of his judgment is come: and worship him that made heaven, and earth, and the sea, and the fountains of waters" (verse 7).

It is important, in the great struggle between God and Satan for the allegiance of humankind, that people know what are the issues. The conflict pivots on whether we will recognize God as the Creator. The Sabbath is the sign of that recognition, and all people will be judged on whether they offer that recognition. God does not leave us in doubt. He sends a special angel with a special message to call the attention of everyone to the facts in the case.

Although John sees and hears an angel proclaiming the message, in reality it is people, God's people, who do the preaching. Jesus gave this responsibility to the church: "Go ye therefore, and teach all nations, baptizing them in the name of the Father, and of the Son, and of the Holy Ghost: teaching them to observe all things whatsoever I have commanded you" (Matthew 28:19, 20). God may well have a specific angel in charge of this preaching, however, ready to assist as necessary.

"The hour of his judgment is come." This is the same judgment that Daniel wrote about, when he saw a vision of God sitting on His throne, surrounded by many angels and record books: "The judgment was set, and the books were opened" (Daniel 7:10). This was still future in Daniel's time; it was to take place after the appearance of the "little horn." That power was to be a chief culprit before the judgment.

The judgment was yet future in Paul's day also, for he spoke forcefully to Governor Felix of a "judgment to come" (Acts 24:25). The great prophecy of 2300 days of Daniel 8 and 9, under the figure of the cleansing of the sanctuary, pinpoints A.D. 1844 as the time when the judgment would begin in heaven. Jesus starts with those who have died and examines the cases of all who have had an opportunity to accept the gospel. Have they indeed made Christ their Savior, or were they His in name only? After all, the great antichrist claims to be as God, all the while making war on the people of God. The judgment will clearly reveal the total picture.

According to John, the angel is proclaiming the judgment in the present tense. He is warning of it even as it is in progress. And so it has been in the fulfillment. Some years before 1844, the date's significance was discovered by a large number of preachers and other Bible students, and what has become known as the great Advent movement began. They were mistaken in the locus of the judgment (they thought that it would be here on earth and thus that it indicated the second coming of Jesus), but their calculations as to the timing were well founded. When the subject was restudied, the place of judgment was determined to be in heaven.

On the Day of Atonement in the Hebraic sanctuary, which was the type of the judgment, the cases of the people were decided in the Most Holy Place, in the presence of the Shekinah, not out among the tents of the people. The people did not have to be present—their cases were determined on the basis of whether they had made sacrifice for their sins. And so in the literal judgment. We do not have to be physically present for our cases to come up before God. They will be decided on whether or not we have accepted Christ as our Savior. If we have, He will represent us before the judgment bar of God.

When this aspect of the judgment became clear, many of those who had been part of the great Advent movement continued to preach the judgment, showing that it was now transpiring in heaven. That proclamation, which is even to this day being made throughout the earth, by pen and voice and electronic technology, is a fulfillment of John's vision.

John saw another angel with another message: "Babylon is fallen, is fallen, that great city, because she made all nations drink of the wine of the wrath of her fornication" (Revelation 14:8). This introduces another symbol, one that we should identify carefully, for we will be meeting it many more times in the book of Revelation.

We know that this is not literal Babylon, the city where Daniel lived and worked, for by John's day that city had been moldering in ruins for years. Moreover, in Revelation 17:5 the name is designated as "mystery." That does not mean we cannot understand it, but it does mean that there is more to it than meets the eye. So our problem is to determine what meaning the word conveyed to John.

Babylon was founded by Nimrod shortly after the Flood. From the very first the city stood for rebellion against God. He had told the people to disperse across the earth and populate it. Instead, Nimrod's followers concentrated in the plain of Shinar. Moreover, they elected to build a tower in defiance of the God who had sent the Flood. God met their defiance and confused their language so that they could no longer co-operate with one another. They left off building the tower and scattered. From this the Hebrews called the site of their efforts balal, "Babel," confusion.

Throughout the Old Testament, Babylon was recognized as in opposition to the will of God. Isaiah pictures Lucifer, or Satan, as the real power behind the throne of Babylon (Isaiah 14:4, 12-14). Bab-ilu, the city's name in the Babylonian language, means "gate of the gods." The Babylonian kings believed their gods had given them the right to rule the world (the "divine right of kings" concept is certainly older than the Middle Ages). They further believed that these gods met in their city to carry on their dealings with humans.

Thus Babylon came to have the opposite connotation from Jerusalem, where the Temple of God was. The two cities represented the opposing forces of good and evil. At one point Nebuchadnezzar, king of Babylon, captured Jerusalem and destroyed it. Jerusalem was later rebuilt, but Babylon waned and fell into ruins.

In Jewish literature the name Babylon began to take on the meaning of rebellion against God. Peter and other early Christian writers used it as a pseudonym for Rome. This may have been in part as a way of circumventing critical eyes, but it also indicated how they felt about the power that persecuted them.

With this historical background we can understand that in Revelation the name Babylon represents all apostate religious organizations, from the beginning of time to the end, even as a noble and pure woman represents God's people throughout time.

The angel's message was that "Babylon is fallen." Of course, at any point in time, Babylon, apostate religion, would be fallen in God's eyes. But particularly after the judgment message has sounded, the world should be aware that there is no salvation in these apostate religions. Those religions that teach there is no divine law, that the Sabbath has been abrogated, that even sinful humanity is immortal, that there is no such thing as a judgment—those religions are fallen, and the sooner the people who are in them are aware of the fact and get out, the better.

God allows a certain amount of grace time for people to come to a knowledge of the truth, but there comes a day when patience ends. God gives a warning, and then acts. So it was in Noah's day. People were so wicked that God "repented" that He had made humans and determined to start over. Through Noah He warned the world of a coming flood. For 120 years Noah preached, but in the end only eight people were saved.

God gave Pharaoh an opportunity to let Israel go out from bondage. Moses warned the king with 10 plagues. When Pharaoh still refused, he and every family in Egypt lost their firstborn children. Before God allowed Babylon to come and carry the Jews captive from Jerusalem, He gave repeated warnings through Isaiah and Jeremiah. Before Christ began His active ministry, God sought to prepare the Jewish nation to receive Him by sending them John the Baptist with a message of repentance. And so before God executes the judgment His wisdom has determined upon this world, in mercy He sends the messages of warning we are discussing.

The third warning is more stringent than either of the first two: "The third angel followed them, saying with a loud voice, If any man worship the beast and his image, and receive his mark in his forehead, or in his hand, the same shall drink of the wine of the wrath of God, which is poured out without mixture into the cup of his indignation; and he shall be tormented with fire and brimstone in the presence of the holy angels, and in the presence of the Lamb: and the smoke of their torment ascendeth up for ever and ever: and they have no rest day nor night, who worship the beast and his image, and whosoever receiveth the mark of his name" (Revelation 14:9-11).

It will be noticed right away into what a quandary this puts the people of earth. In the previous chapter we are told that "no man might buy or sell, save he that had the mark, or the name of the beast, or the number of his name" (Revelation 13:17). Further, we are told that "as many as would not worship the image of the beast should be killed" (verse 15). Now we learn that those who do receive the mark of the beast will suffer the vengeance of God. What to do?

This points up the seriousness of the cosmic conflict. On the one hand the name, the character, the reputation, the honor, of God is at stake. He is the Creator, and only those who recognize Him as such have any place in His universe. On the other hand, the devil knows his own existence is on the line. Although he realizes that his death penalty has already been written—Jesus did that at Calvary (see Hebrews 2:14)—he would like to deceive as many as possible, to drag them down with him. His hatred for God is such that he would kill as many of God's people as he can.

So the battle is a fight to the finish. As for us human beings caught in the middle, the consequences are not so hopeless as they may seem. It looks like death either way, no matter which side we may choose. But God's warning of destruction is much more certain than is Satan's. God can protect us from Satan, but Satan cannot protect anyone from the wrath God directs toward evil people. Moreover, even if a person should lose their physical life in the controversy, if they are martyred for their faith, that is not so calamitous as losing one's eternal salvation.

Jesus said that we should "fear not them which kill the body, but are not able to kill the soul: but rather fear him which is able to destroy both soul and body in hell" (Matthew 10:28). So if the question is merely a matter of which way we would rather die, because of allegiance to God or because of allegiance to the enemy of God, the answer should be clear. But of course that is a negative view of the whole question. Our loyalty to God should be so complete that we will follow Him in everything, no matter what happens. The spirit of Job is commendable: "Though he slay me, yet will I trust in him" (Job 13:15).

In fact, that is the very spirit the redeemed ones will have, those who refuse to bow the knee to the beast or to his image, who refuse to receive the mark. Immediately after giving his warning, the third angel announces, "Here is the patience of the saints: here are they that keep the commandments of God, and the faith of Jesus" (Revelation 14:12). Once again the true people of God in the last days are identified: they are the ones who continue to keep God's commandments, as opposed to the commandments of humans.

The commandments are God's standard. They are the means by which we may know how He wants us to live, what is pleasing to Him. The commandments are based on love—the first four call from us love for God, and the last six characterize our relationship of love toward our fellow humans. God is love, and when we relate to that love in the proper way, we will be in a loving relationship with God and with all the creatures who owe their existence to Him. This is the way Jesus related to the Ten

Commandments, and when we love Jesus, we will love as He loved; we will obey as He obeyed.

The messages of the three angels constitute God's last warning to earth. John says, "I looked, and behold a white cloud, and upon the cloud one sat like unto the Son of man, having on his head a golden crown, and in his hand a sharp sickle" (verse 14). Jesus had told a parable of the harvest. He said, "The harvest is the end of the world. . . . The Son of man shall send forth his angels, and they shall gather out of his kingdom all things that offend, and them which do iniquity; and shall cast them into a furnace of fire: there shall be wailing and gnashing of teeth" (Matthew 13:39-42).

Jesus said that while the tares, or weeds, would be burned, the wheat would be gathered into barns. Harvest speaks of a ripening of the crop and the separation of what is good from what is bad. As the great controversy draws to a climax, the polarization of earth's peoples will become complete. The demarcation between God's true people and those who only profess will be much more clear than may now be the case. But even so, God knows who are His, and He makes no mistakes.

According to the rapture theory and some other concepts of last-day events, when Christ comes He will establish His reign on earth, and everyone, including those who have been in rebellion against Him, will be won over to His side and will acquiesce to His rule. But that is not the picture the Bible gives. Before Jesus returns everyone will have made a decision as to which side he or she is on. The judgment will close on that decision, and Jesus will come and reap the earth accordingly. Surely, as Paul said, "Now is the day of salvation" (2 Corinthians 6:2); now is the time when we hear God's pleading, His warning call, to make our decision to be loyal to Him.

THE SEVEN PLAGUES OF PROPHECY

IN THE last of His three great messages to humanity, God warned against receiving the mark of the beast. Those who receive it, that is, those who persist in paying allegiance to the power that opposes God—specifically, those who continue to honor Sunday, a false day of worship, knowing that God's sign of allegiance is the Sabbath—will be made to "drink of the wine of the wrath of God" (Revelation 14:10).

To some this may seem arbitrary. God has been presented as so loving and kind, so forgiving, that He would never raise a finger against anyone. Of course, God is loving and long-suffering. But justice is as much a part of His character as is mercy. Justice demands an end to sin. Sin brings suffering and pain, and God cannot be just to His creatures without doing something about the cause of their hurt. And so He will destroy sin. This means the destruction as well of those who persist in clinging to sin.

In looking upon the earth in Noah's day, God saw that "the wickedness of man was great in the earth, and that every imagination of the thoughts of his heart was only evil continually" (Genesis 6:5). And so He said, "My spirit shall not always strive with man" (verse 3).

The same situation holds in the last days. God has allowed sin its reign long enough. The reason He did not immediately destroy Satan when he introduced rebellion into the universe is He realized that His creatures, never having seen sin before, did not understand its nature. Had He destroyed Satan (as He had every right to do), other beings would have been afraid of Him. He did not want that kind of universe, and so He allowed sin to demonstrate its true nature.

But one of Satan's accusations against God is that His law is impossible to keep. And so God has allowed time to continue long enough for a significant number of people to demonstrate that, through Jesus Christ, they can live holy, obedient lives. Finally, God will demonstrate that those who are lost would never have repented and come to His side. This is at least one of the reasons for the seven last plagues, the subject of chapters 15 and 16 of Revelation.

In vision John saw a temple in heaven. It is the one after which Moses patterned his tabernacle in the desert. This heavenly temple is where Jesus carries on His work as high priest; it is where the heavenly day of atonement is held, the great judgment.

John saw seven angels come out of the temple, each carrying a golden bowl "full of the wrath of God" (Revelation 15:7). He heard a "great voice" (Revelation 16:1) follow them from the temple, no doubt the voice of God Himself, telling the angels to pour out the contents of their bowls upon the earth. And then John says he saw the temple filled with smoke, and "no man [no person] was able to enter into the temple, till the seven plagues of the seven

97

angels were fulfilled" (Revelation 15:8). Saying that no one was in the temple during this time is to say that Jesus would no longer be carrying on His mediatorial work there; no sins are being forgiven at that time. The judgment will have come to a close; all cases will have been decided. The destiny of all people will be sealed, though they do not know it at the time.

The first angel pours out the contents of his bowl upon the earth, and "there fell a noisome and grievous sore upon the men which had the mark of the beast, and upon them which worshipped his image" (Revelation 16:2). The second angel poured out his bowl upon the sea, "and it became as the blood of a dead man" (verse 3). The third angel emptied his bowl into the streams and rivers, and they too became as blood.

One wonders, Are these real, literal plagues? So far, there is no reason to assume otherwise. God certainly has power over the water. He brought similar plagues against the Egyptians when they refused to free the children of Israel. These plagues are hardly universal, however, for they happen in sequence; if they were universal, there would be no one left alive to suffer the final plagues.

An angel acclaims the fitness of the plagues upon those who have the mark of the beast and who worship the beast's image. "They have shed the blood of saints and prophets," he says (verse 6). We are reminded that the agencies represented by the two beasts of Revelation 13 array themselves against the people of God. They make a decree that as many as would not worship the beast and his image should be killed. These plagues, then, come just in time to deliver God's people from those who have the mark.

Remember the quandary that people must find

themselves in—whether to accept the mark, escape the wrath of the beast, but stand under the wrath of God, or to refuse the mark, stand under the anger of the beast, but escape the wrath of God? The sixteenth chapter shows us that God "gets there first." There may be a few advance skirmishes; some of God's people may indeed lose their lives in the preliminaries; but before the power represented by the beast can execute its universal decree, God preempts the field.

The fourth angel pours out his bowl upon the sun; it intensifies its heat "to scorch men with fire" (verse 8). Now notice what happens. God often allows trials to come to people in order to bring them to Him. "As many as I love, I rebuke and chasten" (Revelation 3:19). But these people upon whom the plagues fall are beyond help. Neither pleading nor chastening will arrest their course. They "blasphemed the name of God . . . and they repented not to give him glory" (Revelation 16:9).

The fifth plague is concentrated upon the "seat of the beast," the capital city and perhaps the centers of influence of the Papacy (verse 10). It is a plague of darkness; some have suggested it indicates the withdrawal of the heat of the sun, as well as its light. Intense cold can be as painful as intense heat.

Again the recipients of this plague blaspheme God. They are still suffering from the sores of the first plague, and many are experiencing the lack of proper water as well. But their attitude shows that there is no way of reaching them; there is no contrition, no repentance. God is justified in ending their existence.

It has been noted that by this end-time, the peoples of the world are polarized into two distinct camps. Those who are on God's side are clearly defined; those who oppose God are equally obvious.

What God decides in judgment in heaven by examining the record books is confirmed on earth by the acts of the people themselves. When God harvests the earth, there will be no doubt as to who are the "wheat" and who are the "tares."

The sixth angel empties his bowl "upon the great river Euphrates; and the water thereof was dried up" (verse 12). Reading only that far, this does not seem so serious a plague. But the following verses show that it is the prologue to "the battle of the great day of God Almighty" (verse 14). John sees three "unclean spirits" come out of the mouths of the dragon, the beast, and the false prophet (verse 13). The kings of the earth are gathered to the great battle, "into a place called in the Hebrew tongue Armageddon" (verse 16).

Is this plague literal like the ones preceding it? It must be noted that the previous plagues have elements of symbolism about them, for they fall upon the "beast" and those who have his "mark." These are symbols, although the plagues themselves may be quite literal.

Similarly there are elements about the sixth plague that are definitely symbolic. John himself says the three spirits "like frogs" are actually the spirits of devils. The dragon is Satan. The drying up of the Euphrates is explained as preparing the way for "the kings of the east" (verse 12), but the literal river Euphrates is not all that great; certainly it would be no deterrent to today's armies.

So we should try to determine the meaning of these symbols. The river Euphrates was the main support of the city of Babylon in ancient times. In Revelation, Babylon represents the apostate religious systems of the world, those religions that oppose God, even as ancient Babylon opposed Jerusalem, the city of God. And so the Euphrates in symbolism could represent some source of support for these religions. Water in prophetic symbolism represents "peoples, and multitudes, and nations, and tongues" (Revelation 17:15). Thus drying of the river Euphrates must bespeak a shriveling of support for these apostate religions.

As for the three "unclean spirits like frogs," we know they are spirits of devils. They come from three sources: the mouth of the dragon, or Satan (this would relate to spiritism); the mouth of the beast, or the Papacy, as is clear from a study of Revelation 13 in conjunction with Daniel 7; and the mouth of the false prophet, or apostate Protestantism, that body of religion that supposedly protests the doctrines and principles of the Papacy but actually follows it in many respects, such as Sunday worship, the doctrine of immortality of the soul, etc.

These spirits "go forth unto the kings of the earth and of the whole world, to gather them to the battle" (Revelation 16:14). That is what Satan has been trying to do all along, to put all the nations of earth, especially their governments, completely under his control. Now he concentrates their forces against God.

Where is this battle? John says the nations of earth are gathered "into a place called in the Hebrew tongue Armageddon." No actual place with such a name has ever been identified, either in contemporary geography or in history. Careful Bible students are not sure what *Armageddon* means. John wrote in Greek, but he transliterated this word from the Hebrew. And that is where the problem arises: What was the original Hebrew word, or words?

The best Greek manuscripts indicate that *Armageddon* combines two Hebrew words. The first one might be *ir,* "city," or more likely *har,* "mountain." But some ancient manuscripts omit this syllable altogether.

The second Hebrew word might be *megiddo*. There was an ancient city by that name situated near an important pass in what is now northern Israel. If this is where John meant, he is perhaps implying a physical battle to take place there. But there is no *mountain* of Megiddo; besides, the other place names of this prophecy—Babylon, Euphrates—are symbolic, and so this may well be, also.

This second Hebrew word in *Armageddon* might be derived from *mo'ed,* "assembly." The Hebrew *harmo'ed* is found in Isaiah 14:13 where Lucifer, or Satan, is described as trying to usurp God's seat of government, the "mount of the congregation." The battle of Armageddon is the "battle of that great day of God Almighty," the climax of the great controversy between God and Satan, and so this latter meaning might be closer to what John had in mind, and not a reference to a geographical place at all.

Note that the sixth plague is not the battle itself but is preparation for the battle. The battle of that great day of God Almighty comes under the seventh plague. The seventh angel pours out his bowl into the air, a voice from the heavenly temple says, "It is done," and there is a great earthquake. "The great city," Babylon, figures again. She receives "the cup of the wine of the fierceness" of God's wrath (Revelation 16:19). The islands and the mountains are moved out of their place by the earthquake, and there is a great hailstorm in which the hailstones weigh as much as 66 pounds each. And again the people blaspheme God.

This last plague is God's last blow in the great controversy. It comes just as the rebellious people make ready to rush upon the commandment keepers to put them to death. God says, "It is done." There is no more reason to prolong the conflict. The final evidence is in. It is time to wind up court.

Right here we should stop to consider the relationship of the people of God to this period of trouble. One of the tenets of those who teach the secret rapture is that the church will escape "the tribulation" by having been transported out of this world before it occurs. This school of thought assigns "the tribulation" to a seven-year period between a supposed secret coming of Christ and His public appearing. All the problems involving the antichrist, including all the persecuting by that power, plus all the plagues, are seen as falling on the earth after the church has left it. Some rapturists understand the catastrophes of the seven seals and the seven trumpets as occurring during this same time.

As for a secret, invisible coming of Christ, we have noted that not once in all the Bible is such an event spoken of or even alluded to. Regarding the seven-year period, we have noted the incongruity of separating it from the other 69 "weeks" of Daniel 9. Now, what about "the tribulation"? Where will the church be during that time?

First, we should note that there are several "tribulation" periods. There was one when Titus besieged Jerusalem. Many inside the city starved to death, and many were killed with the sword. Christians escaped this tribulation, because after threatening the city Titus withdrew for a time. The Christians took this as the sign Jesus had foretold; they left the city before Titus returned and destroyed it.

Christians suffered tribulation under the Roman emperors. Those who would not worship the emperor as a god paid for their faith with their lives. Nero was a particularly rapacious man; so was Diocletian. The lions of the arena claimed many

Christians during these times. But the faith survived.

The period of papal dominance was another time of great tribulation. This is the period referred to in Revelation 13. Millions of dissenters were burned, or pulled apart, or otherwise met violent deaths as martyrs to their faith. But the blood of these martyrs bore fruit in the Reformation.

The situation under the seven last plagues is different. They fall on those who bear the mark of the beast, not upon the church. But the church is still on earth at that time, for it is only after the plagues that Jesus comes to reap the "wheat" and the "tares."

This will be a time of trouble for the people of God, however. The wicked upon whom the plagues fall will blame God and His people for the plagues; they will seek to kill those whom they consider the cause of all their troubles. But God does not allow His people to perish. "And at that time shall Michael stand up, the great prince which standeth for the children of thy people: and there shall be a time of trouble, such as never was since there was a nation even to that same time: and at that time thy people shall be delivered, every one that shall be found written in the book" (Daniel 12:1).

Nothing would be served by the sacrifice of the lives of saints during the seven last plagues. During the Roman persecutions, both pagan and papal, the deaths of Christians often influenced others to take their stand on the side of Christ. But when the plagues fall, humanity's probation will have closed. Christ will have ceased His ministry in the heavenly temple. No additional names will be added to the book of life.

As Christ closes off His mediatorial work, He announces, "He that is unjust, let him be unjust still: and he which is filthy, let him be filthy still: and he that is righteous, let him be righteous still: and he that is holy, let him be holy still. And, behold, I come quickly; and my reward is with me, to give every man according as his work shall be" (Revelation 22:11, 12).

Some proponents of the secret rapture theory claim Luke 21:36 as a promise the church will escape "the tribulation." The text reads, "Watch ye therefore, and pray always, that ye may be accounted worthy to escape all these things that shall come to pass, and to stand before the Son of man." But to be removed bodily from the world is not the only way to escape tribulation. The Israelites were in Egypt during the 10 plagues, yet none of the final seven plagues touched them. Similarly, Daniel's three friends were unharmed while inside Nebuchadnezzar's furnace.

More recent translations of Luke 21:36, based on the best Greek manuscripts, have "that you may have strength to escape" (RSV), or "praying at all times for strength to pass safely through all these imminent troubles" (NEB).

To make sure that we understand the issues in the great cosmic controversy and who the antagonist is, the prophet John has a detailed vision of "Babylon."

In vision he sees a woman riding on a beast. We are reminded of the woman of chapter 12, a noble woman who gave birth to the Christ child. That woman represented God's church, His true people. But the woman John now sees is not pure. She is a harlot, and is dressed typically—in bright colors, decked with much ornamentation. In her hand she has a cup "full of abominations and filthiness of her fornication" (Revelation 17:4).

There can be no mistaking the identity of this woman, for she bears the name in her forehead, "MYS-

TERY, BABYLON THE GREAT, THE MOTHER OF HARLOTS AND ABOMINATIONS OF THE EARTH" (verse 5). Moreover, John saw that she was drunk with the blood of saints and martyrs of Jesus.

Now, if a noble woman represents God's true church, an immoral woman clearly represents religious apostasy. This is borne out in the prophecy of Hosea, in the Old Testament. This man took a wife who proved unfaithful to him. Later he found her in the slave market and bought her back. God used that as a parable of His experience with Israel. She had been unfaithful in her relationship with God; she had played the harlot with the false gods of the nations around her. At that time God was willing to take Israel back, but later He told her He was through (Matthew 21:43; 23:38). Here in Revelation the figure of a harlot represents all apostate religions.

This woman is sitting on a beast that has familiar features—it has seven heads and ten horns, is "full of names of blasphemy" (Revelation 17:3), and all the world wonders after it. This, of course, is the beast of Revelation 13. The seven heads are identified as seven kings, or the various phases in which Satan has manifested his power and enmity against God—beginning with Egypt and culminating in the Papacy, which in John's day "is not yet come" (Revelation 17:10). The seven mountains may reflect the same meaning as the seven kings, or they may be an allusion to the City of Seven Hills, Rome.

Although the woman is riding on a beast, she is also figured as sitting on "waters" (verses 1, 15). In the thirteenth chapter the beast itself is viewed as rising from waters. And so the picture is the same—the beast is a universal power, in that it derives its strength from "peoples, and multitudes, and nations, and tongues." Similarly, the woman is also universal, and she derives direct support from the beast.

The kings of the earth lend their support to this apostate religious system, and together they make war with the Lamb. What a picture of the uniting of the powers of church and state! But they are fighting against God, and God will prevail, "for he is Lord of lords, and King of kings: and they that are with him are called, and chosen, and faithful" (verse 14).

This is the situation in the battle of Armageddon. Regardless of whether a specific, literal background is described, the key fact is that it is a battle between Satan and his forces and God and His forces.

There are those who see Satan as a necessary element in the grand scheme of things. They feel that evil is a required balance of good, that God needs a devil against which to compare Himself; or, for those who believe in an eternally burning hell, they see Satan as maintaining a necessary post, even as sanitation engineers are required for an efficiently operating city. Nothing could be further from the truth! Sin is an aberration, a blot on the universe, a contradiction of God. Light and darkness cannot coexist, truth and error are incompatible. And so Satan must go.

Again the cry comes from heaven, "Babylon the great is fallen, is fallen, and is become the habitation of devils," and the appeal is made, "Come out of her, my people, that ye be not partakers of her sins, and that ye receive not of her plagues" (Revelation 18:2, 4). Today, before the plagues fall, some of God's people are in Babylon. They have not known the issues that are at stake in the great controversy—they have not known that there is a Babylon, or that they are in it! But their hearts are true to God. They love Him sincerely and they want to do what is right. God knows their hearts, but He also knows what is going to happen to Babylon, to the apostate religions. And so He is calling His people to come out before it is too late.

Traditional religion, or how our parents believed, or what the majority of the churches teach, is no criterion of truth. What matters is "what saith the Lord?" If we should find our church in opposition to what the Lord commands, then there is only one thing to do—come out.

The plagues will come upon Babylon suddenly, unexpectedly—"in one day"; "in one hour," John says (verses 8, 10). The irrevocable sentence will have been passed in heaven, but Babylon will not know it until too late. And so we cannot expect to wait until the plagues fall to make our decision. That will be beyond the point of no return.

The author of the Epistle to the Hebrews asks, "How shall we escape, if we neglect so great salvation; which at the first began to be spoken by the Lord, and was confirmed unto us by them that heard him?" "Take heed, brethren, lest there be in any of you an evil heart of unbelief, in departing from the living God. But exhort one another daily, while it is called To day; lest any of you be hardened through the deceitfulness of sin" (Hebrews. 2:3; 3:12, 13).

"And a mighty angel took up a stone like a great millstone, and cast it into the sea, saying, Thus with violence shall that great city Babylon be thrown down, and shall be found no more at all" (Revelation 18:21).

As Babylon, the symbol of the world's apostate religions, is destroyed, John hears all heaven rejoice. It is the culmination of long ages of conflict. The angels who remained loyal to God helped banish Satan and the disloyal angels from heaven (Revelation 12:7-9). They saw Satan gain dominion over this world by deceiving first Eve, then Adam. They witnessed ... evil in this world's history, culminating i... their own beloved Leader on Calvary. The... the ebb and tide of good and evil—the long ... papal dominion and persecution; the Reformation, time of Laodicea, when God's church was lukewarm. They saw the building crescendo that climaxed in the seven last plagues; and now they have seen the destruction of Babylon. The angels have had a share in this great conflict, and now they rejoice in God's triumph.

And not only the angels of heaven. "And I heard as it were the voice of a great multitude, and as the voice of many waters, and as the voice of mighty thunderings, saying, Alleluia: for the Lord God omnipotent reigneth" (Revelation 19:6). Many references are made in the Bible to other intelligent beings whom God has created, who populate other worlds. (See Job 1:6; Ephesians 3:10-15; Revelation 12:12.) All of these join in the great paean of praise to the Creator.

And now comes the grand event. Now comes the moment for which "the whole creation groaneth and travaileth in pain together until now" (Romans 8:22). Now comes the fruition of "that blessed hope, and the glorious appearing of the great God and our Saviour Jesus Christ" (Titus 2:13).

John sees heaven open. Out steps a white horse, and One sitting on the horse, who is called Faithful and True and The Word of God (Revelation 19:11, 13). His eyes are as flaming fire, and out of His mouth issues a sharp sword. He wears on His head many crowns; correspondingly, His cloke, which has been dipped in blood, bears the insignia, "KING OF KINGS, AND LORD OF LORDS" (verse 16). It is Jesus Christ.

Following Jesus are the armies of heaven, "upon white horses" (verse 14). These armies, of course, are els of God. John sees "the beast, and the kings the earth, and their armies, gathered together to make war against him that sat on the horse, and against his army" (verse 19). It is the "battle of that great day of God Almighty."

This is but another version of the great second coming of Jesus Christ. Jesus described it variously as like the return of a householder from a far country, like a farmer harvesting his grain, like a king's son taking a bride. But He made clear that His return would be very literal. "I will come again," He said. "They shall see the Son of man coming in the clouds of heaven with power and great glory. And he shall send his angels with a great sound of a trumpet, and they shall gather together his elect from the four winds" (Matthew 24:30, 31).

At His coming He will be just as real as when He left this earth. Declared the angels then, "This same Jesus, which is taken up from you into heaven, shall so come in like manner as ye have seen him go into heaven" (Acts 1:11).

As Christ appears in the sky, accompanied by all of heaven's glorious angels, the earth erupts in violent earthquakes; fires break out and destroy the cities; mountains topple into the sea; islands disappear; graves are opened, and the redeemed who died in the faith of Jesus are resurrected to watch their King approach; the unrepentant stand aghast at the sight of the One they have rejected, and try to hide from Him. It is the answer to the prayer of faithful ones down through the ages: "Our Father which art in heaven, Hallowed be thy name. Thy kingdom come. . . . Deliver us from evil: For thine is the kingdom, and the power, and the glory, for ever. Amen" (Matthew 6:9-13).

THE SIGNS
ALL FORETELL

IN ANY study of the Second Coming, the one question that clamors for attention is When? "When will Christ come?" the skeptic asks in derision. "When will Christ come?" the weary saint asks, impatient in a world gone mad.

In promising His return, Jesus could not tell His disciples all the details of their future. It would be too much for them to bear. But He said the Holy Spirit would reveal to them what they needed to know, as that need arose.

From His statements regarding the signs of His return, especially those recorded in Matthew 24 that are tied in with the omens of Jerusalem's destruction, His followers deduced that He would return during their lifetime. Indeed, did He not use the personal pronoun? "I will come again, and receive you unto myself" (John 14:3). So Paul, under the inspiration of the Holy Spirit, had to throw in a word of caution: "That day shall not come, except there come a falling away first, and that man of sin be revealed, the son of perdition" (2 Thessalonians 2:3).

Even so, the early church did not dream that centuries would elapse. Elderly John, the last survivor of the original 12 disciples, may have had an inkling, from the visions given him on Patmos, that much was yet to happen before the final end of sin. But what he was told to write was couched in such terms as not to discourage the church in the ages of persecution.

Was God unfair in presenting before the church the hope of an imminent return? No, hope is one of the three essentials of the human spirit. Hope gives us a goal, direction, purpose. It helps to focus our energies toward victory. Without it, we give up and don't even try. Physicians know that an essential element to recuperation from surgery or some grave disease is the "will to live." This will is based on hope; we must have something to live for, something to look forward to.

Every generation of Christians has expected Jesus to return "soon"—each Christian has hoped to see Jesus face to face before death. Each generation of Jews expected the Messiah, also. Even Eve, to whom the promise was first made, thought that her firstborn son might be the Redeemer.

So God through hope keeps us awake, alert. "Watch," He says.

Jesus' disciples shared a feeling of anxiety. Though a part of their heart expected Jesus to take the throne of Israel immediately, they were beginning to become aware that He might have other plans. He kept talking about going away and coming again. Then, too, there were the prophecies of Scripture that told of a terrible "day of the Lord," a "day of darkness and of gloominess" (Joel 2:1, 2).

When Jesus spoke of the stones of the beloved Temple being cast down, the disciples immediately associated this with the portended end of the world. They asked Jesus, "When shall these things be? and what shall be the sign of thy coming, and of the end of the world?" (Matthew 24:3). They assumed that the destruction of the Temple was to be synonymous with the climax of history.

With broad sweeps Jesus described catastrophes that would unfold as world history—wars, famines, earthquakes, pestilence, religious persecution. Then He went on to the triumph of the gospel and His own return in glory. As the disciples had thrown together, in their question, the destruction of the Temple and the end of the world, Jesus included both events in His reply. The disciples—and the church—must be prepared for the here and now, as well as for the hereafter. The kingdom of heaven speaks to the present and personal, as well as to the future and universal.

Not all prophecies, especially those relating to Jesus' coming, are intended to provide for us a time chart. If it were necessary or even desirable for us to know the exact time of His return, or even to know the exact sequence of events leading up to His return, Jesus would have told us. Or the apostles in their subsequent revelations could have spelled it out in more detail. But Jesus said, "It is not for you to know the times or the seasons, which the Father hath put in his own power" (Acts 1:7). In other words, it is not so much that we do not know, or that we cannot know, but it is not our business to know. It is not for our best welfare to know.

Many of the prophecies are given for an altogether different reason. "And now I have told you before it come to pass," Jesus told His disciples after one discussion relative to His going away, "that, when it is come to pass, ye might believe" (John

14:29). After an event has taken place, when we can point to the place in Scripture where that event was foretold, it strengthens our faith in the Word of God and in the God who has the world in His hands.

Of course, with some events, such as the Second Coming itself, it will be too late to wait until the fulfillment and then say, "Oh, so that is what God meant!" The prophecies we do see fulfilling should tell us that the others, the ones we don't fully understand, will be fulfilled just as surely. Hindsight, then, can be as important as foresight in the final account of things.

As we study with this inspired hindsight into the reply of Jesus to the disciples on that day on Mount Olivet, we can see those portions of His remarks that were relevant to the destruction of the Temple. We take particular note of verses 15-20 of Matthew 24. The disciples themselves appropriated the instruction they needed, at the time for which it was intended. As the armies of Titus first surrounded Jerusalem, the Christians inside the city remembered the counsel of Christ. Mysteriously, Titus withdrew his forces for a short time—long enough for the Christians to flee the city. Then Titus renewed his attack, ending in the complete destruction of the Temple and the savage death of a million Jews. But not one Christian lost their life in the conflict.

Most of the remainder of Matthew 24 may be applied to the Second Coming—false christs, the sun and moon darkened, the stars falling. Luke adds that there will be great distress among nations, that people's hearts will fail them for fear.

This apparently was as much as the disciples could absorb at that time, still confused as they were over the possibility of Christ announcing His kingship—perhaps even at the Passover that was coming up. Years later, Paul and Peter and John added to our picture of events and conditions surrounding the subject of Christ's return.

In his first letter to Timothy, Paul described religious conditions in the last days. "Now the Spirit speaketh expressly, that in the latter times some shall depart from the faith, giving heed to seducing spirits, and doctrines of devils; speaking lies in hypocrisy; having their conscience seared with a hot iron" (1 Timothy 4:1, 2). Succeeding verses describe conditions that even in Paul's day were beginning to affect the church.

"The doctrines of devils" in a literal sense is a religious phenomenon typical of our present day. Never before has there been such an interest in the occult. Devil worship and black magic are steadily becoming more popular in the "civilized" world. Spiritists are seen as a synthesizing force between Catholics and Protestants—in fulfillment of prophecy.

In his second letter to his young protégé, Paul referred to social conditions that would prevail "in the last days" (2 Timothy 3:1). "Men shall be lovers of their own selves, covetous, boasters, proud, blasphemers, disobedient to parents, unthankful, unholy, without natural affection, truce-breakers, false accusers, incontinent, fierce, despisers of those that are good, traitors, heady, highminded, lovers of pleasures more than lovers of God; having a form of godliness, but denying the power thereof" (verses 2-5).

Peter tells us that "there shall come in the last days scoffers, walking after their own lusts, and saying, Where is the promise of his coming? for since the fathers fell asleep, all things continue as they were from the beginning of the creation" (2 Peter 3:3, 4). This prophecy certainly can be applied to evolutionists,

115

and even to some so-called theistic evolutionists.

Many of these signs are general and, it can be argued, have been present since the inception of sin—in which case they at least teach that the world will not progressively grow better, up to the coming of Christ. The idea that there will be 1,000 years of peace, prosperity, and general sanctity before Christ reigns is simply not biblical. Instead, we get the picture of a crescendo of lawlessness and apostasy. This is concurrent with an increase in natural disasters, as though the earth itself were groaning with the weight of a rebellious humanity.

Wars have been getting more universal, and more costly in terms of human lives as well as natural resources. Seven million tons of bombs were rained on Southeast Asia in what was officially only a "police action." What the results would have been had that conflict escalated to a "real war" is unthinkable.

One main reason, strategists say, that the major powers have not gone to war ere this is a mutual fear of the consequences of nuclear conflict. But with the proliferation of nuclear potential, that fear and respect is slipping down the drain. With each new nation joining the "nuclear club," the chance of somebody—perhaps a revolutionary terrorist group—triggering a holocaust is multiplied.

The specter of economic disaster, coupled with a worldwide energy crisis, looms as cause aplenty for new outbreaks of war jitters. Confidence in government is at a low ebb. One scandal after another tends to drive people to extremes—they feel prepared to sacrifice liberty for security.

But what of the individual? Are people becoming more enlightened, morally advanced? A woman, despondent over losing her job, climbed a municipal water tower. A crowd of 300 people gathered below. To dissuade her from jumping? To catch her if she jumped? Oh, no! To jeer her and taunt her into jumping! Firemen and police arrived to rescue the woman; the crowd screamed obscenities and threw rocks at them. After the woman had been brought down and put into a patrol car to be taken to the hospital, the crowd smashed the car's windshield.

Another town, another time: a thunderstorm came up suddenly; a young boy ran for shelter; he was hit by lightning. Again a crowd gathered, but not to help the boy. Almost to a person their lament was "I never saw anyone get hit by lightning. I wish I would have been here to see it when it happened."

In a city park vandals capture mallards that live on a pond. They break the birds' legs and throw them back into the water, to laugh at their awkward attempts to swim. Or they tie the ducks in plastic bags, hang them from trees, and beat them to death with sticks.

A million abandoned children swarm through the cities of Latin America. Their parents don't want them; society has no concern for them. Like homeless dogs they live from garbage cans, or from the sale of stolen items. They sleep in unused doorways, under a newspaper for a blanket. And sometimes a prankster will set fire to the newspaper, destroying the life of a homeless waif.

In predicting just such social conditions as these, the apostle Paul contrasts them with the life of the redeemed in the kingdom of God. Christ's coming will put an end to the reign of sin. But Satan realizes his time is short; as a result of his desperation, conditions will get worse before the coming of Christ makes them better.

Perhaps the biggest burden facing this planet today

is overpopulation. This problem spawns, or at least intensifies, many of the others. Parents who have too many mouths to feed push some of their children out to fend for themselves. There is only a limited amount of land available for food and living space. According to an agricultural expert, except for a few million acres set aside by the government in the United States, only Brazil and Africa have tillable land that is not under cultivation. Yet, as the population and the demand for food grow in astronomical proportions, land is gobbled up for housing, highways, and parking lots.

A major science advisory council has warned that unless something drastic is done immediately to curb world population, within 20 years the whole world will be plagued with food shortages and, within 40 years, starvation. The council said the world is about to reach the point of no return, that soon we will reach the place where no matter what we do, it will be too late.

Aggravating the food shortage is the doubling and redoubling of oil prices. Petroleum is used in making commercial fertilizers, in farming crops, and in transporting them to consumers. Another factor is the growing scarcity of water. A former U.S. president warned, "It should be clear now that we are in a race with disaster. Either the world's water needs will be met or the inevitable result will be mass starvation, mass epidemics, and mass poverty greater than anything we know today."

But before the food itself gives out, there will be riots over the food that is still left. In one Southern Asian country grain trains are stopped and looted on their way to drought-stricken areas.

Overpopulation creates other problems than food shortages. The closer people are thrown together, the more they turn to violence and other antisocial acts.

A recent poll showed that each year, one U.S. city dweller out of three is mugged, robbed, or suffers property loss. And the more people there are, the more they foul the planet they share. One source has calculated that within a few years atmospheric pollution alone could kill 90 percent of mankind.

The permissiveness of society in regard to moral standards is definitely a fulfillment of Paul's prophecy to Timothy. There have been sexual excesses since before the Flood, but never so flaunted as today. On billboards, in movies for family viewing, on television and the stage, in family magazines and in newspapers, emphasis is placed on sex and its perversions. Ours is not just an "open" society, but one that is increasingly sex-saturated to the exclusion of other motivations.

And where is the church? Is it holding up the standards of purity and holiness, preparing a people for God's kingdom? Paul said a sign of the last days would be a form of godliness only; people would bear the name of Christian but they would deny the power of a Christlike life. And so we have the news of a church hosting a convention of prostitutes who are organizing to protect their "rights." And another church sponsors jazz sessions, in which a male dancer dances in the nude on stage.

Homosexuality, a word that was not breathed in public a couple of decades ago, now has its public defenders, even in the church. Groups in both Protestant and Catholic churches have made proposals urging the ordination of homosexual priests and ministers. These proposals have succeeded in some areas, and there are entire church congregations made up of avowed homosexuals, Paul's words in Romans 1:24-32 notwithstanding.

The pure in heart are revolted by such things, and

wonder what will be the end of it all. God has His answer—He will destroy evil and establish the world in righteousness. We can rejoice that the signs indicate that that day is near!

Another feature unique to modern society that the devil is using to his own ends is the rapid rate of change. This is tied indirectly to the advance of knowledge. Knowledge snowballs; as soon as a unit of information comes to light in one field, it opens the doors to new discoveries in a dozen other fields, each one of which opens doors in still more areas.

For 6,000 years humanity's fastest speed was that of a horse. In the 1800s, after the invention of the steam locomotive, humans were able to go 100 miles an hour. In only 60 years that speed was multiplied by four by the airplane. After another two decades humans were doubling that speed, now traveling at 800 miles an hour. But it took only one more decade to multiply that by 30 times, for humans could and did travel 24,000 miles an hour as they left earth's atmosphere for the moon.

If one were to take the sum of human knowledge gained over the past 6,000 years, and determine the halfway point, it would fall within the past 50 years. Ninety percent of all the scientists who have ever lived are alive today. Should knowledge continue increasing at its present rate, the total sum of knowledge today represents only 4 percent of what it will be a lifetime (70 years) from now. Most of the medicines on the drugstore shelf today were not available to doctors 10 years ago.

One of the fastest-growing areas of knowledge is that of genetics and biochemistry. In a process called cloning, humans can take a cell of a carrot—any cell, whether from the root or the top—and grow a new carrot. No need for seed. Similarly, they can take a cell of a sheep and grow a new sheep. No need for father or mother. Scientists predict that soon they will be able to grow a new human being from a cell—again, any cell, from finger tip or earlobe. Using that technique, they could multiply a whole generation of Einsteins from one original—or a new generation of Hitlers, depending on the morals of the scientist doing the manipulating.

This rapid increase in knowledge brings with it a rapid change in humanity's environment—often too fast for them to adjust to. "Bring on the new models, throw away the old." "Tear down the almost-new buildings, put up still newer." In one nation the average family moves every nine years. In the city of Washington, D.C., half the families will move in any given year. This flux brings its own psychological burdens—find a new dentist, doctor, pastor, grocer, neighbor, friend. The "throwaway" mentality spawned by fast obsolescence of products extends into the personal life. Now we can have throwaway friends, wives, children. People become flotsam on a sea of change.

They also become drunk with change; they demand more and more. A definite syndrome, or pattern, of emotional responses emerges. An early symptom is the breakdown of mores; this leads to boredom, which breeds violence, riots, revolution. Finally, there is a loss of rational control. This cycle has been demonstrated in laboratory animals and in humans.

Of course, the devil takes advantage of this trend. It plays right into his hand. He uses it as a drug to make the masses plastic to his will.

How thankful we may be that God is the master of change. He is our rock, our steady beacon. He performs change Himself—He makes new creatures of those who yield their sinful selves to Him. Or He can override change. But God Himself changes not. Those who are on His side must be alert to the psychological forces at work about them, ready to counteract as far as possible the demoralizing influences in the world.

All of the above factors, singly or together, signal a sick planet. No one now holds any real hope that humans will be able to improve their own lot here. A Nobel laureate and professor of nuclear physics ventures that not even the scarcity of raw materials will succeed in dismantling armies. Humans intrinsically are combative creatures. "Ultimately, as major resources disappear, we will go at each other with bows and arrows and poleaxes." The best that technologists hope for is that we will be able to send colonies to other planets and start anew there.

But God has other plans for this planet. He created it to be inhabited, not to be left as an empty hulk, unable to support life. That is why He has made provision to end sin, the devil, and all suffering. That is why He has promised to come again. If ever humankind needed the intervention of God, it is now. We have never needed so much to be made over anew, to be set back on the right track.

ONE THOUSAND
YEARS—OF WHAT?

IN MANY respects the twentieth chapter of Revelation is a key to the whole book. Not only does it give an overview of the entire controversy between Christ and Satan: it describes the end of that controversy in particular. It portrays what will happen to Satan and his forces, and reveals what will happen to the faithful people of God. Moreover, this chapter affords a chronological sequence to some important events.

Although the subject matter covered is broad, the chapter itself is brief, so we will have to round out our understanding of the topics by referring to passages in other places of the Bible.

First, we note that the opening topic of this chapter comes right on the heels of the coming of Christ as king, and the destruction of the beast and those who worship him. We should be particularly aware of the circumstances that coincide with that great event.

As Christ comes, both His people and His enemies will be living on earth. He announces that His reward is with Him, to give to each person as he or she deserves (Revelation 22:11, 12). That passage identifies the "unjust" and the "filthy" on the one hand, the "righteous" and the "holy" on the other. For brevity, we will use in this discussion the terms "wicked" and "righteous."

John describes Jesus as coming on a white horse, with a sharp sword issuing from His mouth; he also speaks of Him as carrying a sharp sickle. While the coming is literal, the sword and the sickle are no doubt figurative, to emphasize both the conquering nature of His coming and the reaping nature. Other passages are as descriptive but without these dramatic figures.

In Revelation 1:7 we read He will come with clouds and that every eye shall see Him. It is, then, a public, well-publicized appearing. John also says that those who participated in Jesus' crucifixion will witness His return. This is in harmony with what Jesus Himself told the high priest at His trial, "Hereafter shall ye see the Son of man sitting on the right hand of power, and coming in the clouds of heaven" (Matthew 26:64). Apparently there will be a special resurrection of these people so that they might see just who it was they crucified.

These clouds may be literal clouds, they may be the billows of glory that accompany Christ, or the phrase may refer to the myriads of heavenly angels that come with Him. His coming will be as startling, as forceful, and as pronounced as lightning.

Jesus will come literally and in bodily form. When He left His disciples from Mount Olivet, He was a human being, albeit a divine human being. He was God, and He was also man. He had flesh, He ate food, He had a recognizable form. As He left, He arose into the air, was taken into a cloud, and disappeared. Two angels appeared to the disciples who watched Him go, and said, "This same Jesus, which is taken up from you into heaven, shall so come in like manner as ye have seen him go into heaven" (Acts 1:11).

We have already noted that the coming of Christ spells death for the wicked. Some call for the rocks and the mountains to fall on them and hide them from the face of Jesus (Revelation 6:15-17). Others are slain by the brightness of His coming (2 Thessalonians 2:8). If any remain, defiant to the last, they are slain outright. "And the remnant were slain with the sword of him that sat upon the horse, which sword proceedeth out of his mouth; and all the fowls were filled with their flesh" (Revelation 19:21).

But for the righteous the picture is different. For them it is the great moment of deliverance. Only a short time before, they had stood in danger of their lives before the hosts of the wicked, who had the mark of the beast and demanded that these receive it as well. Just in time Jesus, their deliverer, comes. "And it shall be said in that day, Lo, this is our God; we have waited for him, and he will save us: this is the Lord; we have waited for him, we will be glad and rejoice in his salvation" (Isaiah 25:9).

Picture the awful situation at this moment. It is not only the threats of the wicked that have been hanging over the heads of these people. On every hand they have been witnessing the effects of the seven plagues—water turned to blood, great heat, extreme darkness and probably attending cold, the hailstorm, great earthquakes, cities destroyed, thunders, lightnings, islands moved out of place, mountains shifting around, even heaven itself opening and closing as a scroll.

Then, just as these righteous people reach their extremity, even as the weapons of the wicked are raised against them, there appears in the heavens "the sign of the Son of man" (Matthew 24:30). The wicked are stopped in their tracks, their faces frozen in horror. The trumpet of God sounds, the "voice of the archangel," and these wicked fall dead.

This trumpet of God has a wonderful effect on the earth. Graves break open in many places, and those who have died righteous are raised to life. "The Lord himself shall descend from heaven with a shout, with the voice of the archangel, and with the trump of God: and the dead in Christ shall rise first" (1 Thessalonians 4:16).

Those who have died as Christians since the death of Christ are raised, as well as all who have ever lived who believed the Messiah was their salvation. "Your father Abraham rejoiced to see my day," Jesus said. "And he saw it, and was glad" (John 8:56). The entire eleventh chapter of Hebrews teaches that the faithful of old will be saved by their faith, even as we are. God does not have many ways of saving people; in fact, He has only one—through Jesus Christ. People may understand much of that plan, or little, but according to their faith shall be their reward. And so "he shall send his angels with a great sound of a trumpet, and they shall gather together his elect from the four winds, from one end of heaven to the other" (Matthew 24:31).

As these people are raised from the dead, their bodies are changed. They will continue to have bodies; they will be recognizable to each other, even as Jesus was after His resurrection; but their bodies will be of a different nature. They will now be immortal. "The trumpet shall sound, and the dead shall be raised incorruptible, and we shall be changed. For this corruptible must put on incorruption, and this mortal must put on immortality" (1 Corinthians 15:52, 53).

And not only the dead will be changed at this moment. Those righteous who are living when Jesus returns will also receive immortal bodies: "We shall not all sleep, but we shall all be changed" (verse 51). "For our conversation [manner of living] is in heaven; from whence also we look for the Saviour, the Lord Jesus Christ: who shall change our vile body, that it may be fashioned like unto his glorious body" (Philippians 3:20, 21).

Right here it should be noted that this is the first time that the saints actually possess immortality. Immortality is promised in Jesus, and when we accept Him as our life we have eternal life, but it remains in His keeping until He comes. Until that time, only He has it! "The blessed and only Potentate, the King of kings, and Lord of lords; who only hath immortality" (1 Timothy 6:15, 16). As for the wicked, they never have had it and never will: "God hath given to us eternal life, and this life is in his Son. He that hath the Son hath life; and he that hath not the Son of God hath not life" (1 John 5:11, 12).

That humanity inherently possesses an immortal soul is the first lie Satan ever told on earth (Genesis 3:4). It is part of the "wine" of false doctrines with which the harlot Babylon fills her cup. The wages of sin is death, not immortality. If humanity already had immortality, Jesus need not have died, "for God so loved the world, that he gave his only begotten Son, that whosoever believeth in him should not perish, but have everlasting life" (John 3:16).

Immortality is the reward for the righteous that Jesus brings with Him when He comes. "He that overcometh," Jesus says, "shall not be hurt of the second death" (Revelation 2:11).

The righteous who have been raised from their graves, along with the righteous who have remained alive, will be caught up to meet Jesus Christ, "and so shall we ever be with the Lord" (1 Thessalonians 4:17). This is the rapture, or translation, of the saints. But note that there is nothing secret about it, nothing invisible, nothing silent, and it takes place at the public, glorious, triumphant appearing of our Lord.

What happens to the righteous at this point? Paul says they are caught up to meet the Lord and they remain with Him. Jesus made the promise, "I go to prepare a place for you. And if I go and prepare a place for you, I will come again, and receive you unto myself; that where I am there ye may be also" (John 14:2, 3). That indicates clearly that Jesus will take the righteous back to heaven with Him.

And indeed that is where John several times in vision saw the righteous. "I beheld, and, lo, a great multitude, which no man could number, of all nations, and kindreds, and people, and tongues, stood before the throne, and before the Lamb, clothed with white robes, and palms in their hands" (Revelation 7:9). "And I saw as it were a sea of glass mingled with fire: and them that had gotten the victory over the beast, and over his image, and over his mark, and over the number of his name, stand on the sea of glass, having the harps of God" (Revelation 15:2).

Consider what condition this leaves the earth in. The wicked are all dead; they were killed at the coming of the Lord. The righteous are all gone, taken to heaven by Christ, according to His promise. The cities of earth are desolate, destroyed by the earthquakes, fires, and hailstorm.

How aptly these words from Isaiah describe the condition that will prevail: "Behold, the Lord maketh the earth empty, and maketh it waste, and turneth it upside down, and scattereth abroad the inhabitants thereof. . . . The land shall be utterly emptied, and utterly spoiled. . . . The earth also is defiled under the inhabitants thereof; because they have transgressed the laws, changed the ordinance, broken the everlasting covenant." "The earth is utterly broken down, the earth is clean dissolved, the earth is moved exceedingly. The earth shall reel to and fro like a drunkard, and shall be removed like a cottage; and the transgression thereof shall be heavy upon it; and it shall fall, and not rise again" (Isaiah 24:1-5, 19, 20).

Jeremiah has a similar description: "I beheld the earth, and, lo, it was without form, and void; and the heavens, and they had no light. I beheld the mountains, and, lo, they trembled, and all the hills moved lightly. I beheld, and, lo, there was no man, and all the birds of the heavens were fled. I beheld, and, lo, the fruitful place was a wilderness, and all the cities thereof were broken down at the presence of the Lord, and by his fierce anger" (Jeremiah 4:23-26).

Now we are ready to take up our study of Revelation 20, which picks up the narrative at the point of Jesus' triumphal appearing. John says he saw an angel come down from heaven with a great chain in his hand. He casts the devil, Satan, into the "bottomless pit" (Revelation 20:1) and shuts him up and sets a seal on him. He cannot deceive the nations for 1,000 years. After the 1,000 years are over, he is released for "a little season" (verse 3).

Satan cannot deceive the nations because there is no one to deceive! The wicked are all dead, and the righteous are all gone. Satan is left alone—only he and his evil angels. He cannot leave this earth; he is bound to it. And indeed it is certainly like a bottomless pit—bodies of the wicked strewn all about, the cities broken down, fruitful places a wilderness. Even the topography of the earth is a frightful mess, a result of the great earthquake.

So for 1,000 years Satan is left to contemplate the state to which he has brought the world, the wicked, the rebellious angels, and himself. He has nothing else to do, and he cannot leave. God has "set a seal" upon him (verse 3). Ironically, he had once set a seal upon God. When Jesus was in the tomb, Satan tried to keep Him there. He instigated the leaders to set a Roman guard at the tomb, and to put a Roman seal on the stone that blocked the door. No one dared to break that seal, but it meant nothing to the angels who came to call Jesus forth from the dead. Now the tables are turned; Satan has the seal upon him.

Nor is this the kind of seal that marks the righteous, described in Revelation 7. That is a seal of allegiance to God, and it becomes a seal of deliverance by God. Satan is marked with a seal for destruction. He knows it, and he trembles.

And what of the righteous? How are they occupied? John records, "I saw thrones, and they sat upon them, and judgment was given unto them: . . . and they lived and reigned with Christ a thousand years" (Revelation 20:4).

Thrones indicate rulership or authority of some kind. The text says the responsibility of judgment is given to the saints. How is this? Is not Christ the judge? Does not He decide every case before He comes to earth? Who is there for the saints to judge during the millennium?

We should bear in mind that there are several kinds of judgment. One is the investigative kind, when determination is made as to right and wrong, or who is right and who is wrong. Obviously, only God can make that kind of judgment, and that is the kind Christ is making now, prior to His coming. Another kind of judgment is when sentence is passed, when the determination is made as to how much punishment and what kind shall be meted to the guilty. A third kind of judgment is when the sentence is actually carried out, when it is executed. Still another kind is when someone reviews the evidence and determines that the sentence is just.

Paul asks, "Do ye not know that the saints shall judge the world? . . . Know ye not that we shall judge angels?" (1 Corinthians 6:2, 3). God having determined who is righteous and who is guilty, it will be in the hands of the saints, as they sit on thrones of judgment, to determine what the sentence shall be. Moreover—and this is important—the saints will have opportunity to review every case. Thus they can assure themselves that God has been just with every person. There need never be a doubt, throughout the eons of eternity, that God has made a mistake, that justice has misfired. There will never be an excuse for doubting God.

What happens at the close of the 1,000 years? John continues, "When the thousand years are expired, Satan shall be loosed out of his prison" (Revelation 20:7). Since he is imprisoned by being deprived of anyone to tempt, his loosening implies that he again has someone to tempt. In other words, there will be a return of some of those who had lived on earth previously. These are not the righteous, because they are forever beyond the reach of the devil. The implication is that the wicked are raised to life again. The same implication is found in verse 5: "But the rest of the dead [that is, those who are not in heaven living and reigning with Jesus, i.e., the wicked] lived not again until the thousand years were finished." The conclusion is that when the 1,000 years are finished, the "rest of the dead," the wicked, do live again.

That the wicked are raised in a resurrection of their own is clearly taught by Daniel, Jesus, and Paul. "Many of them that sleep in the dust of the earth shall awake, some to everlasting life, and some to shame and everlasting contempt" (Daniel 12:2). "There shall be a resurrection of the dead, both of the just and unjust" (Acts 24:15). Jesus delineated these as two distinct resurrections: "The hour is coming, in the which all that are in the graves shall hear his voice, and shall come forth; they that have done good, unto the resurrection of life; and they that have done evil, unto the resurrection of damnation" (John 5:28, 29).

John avers that the first resurrection is for the righteous: "Blessed and holy is he that hath part in the first resurrection" (Revelation 20:6). If this is stipulated as the "first," that in itself indicates there is a second. Moreover, John declares that the wicked suffer the "second death" (verses 6, 14). Everyone, good or bad, is subject to one death. But the wicked suffer a second death. In order to do that, there must be an intervening resurrection.

This, then, is what releases Satan at the end of the 1,000-year period. The wicked are raised, not to eternal life, but to shame and contempt. Satan goes out to deceive them once again, and this time there is no deterrent to his wiles. There is no Holy Spirit pleading with these people to obey God; there are no righteous among them to prick their consciences. They follow Satan completely. And there are myriads of them, "the number of whom is as the sand of the sea" (verse 8). All the wicked who have ever lived, who died outside the pale of salvation, are here in Satan's hands.

"They went up on the breadth of the earth, and compassed the camp of the saints about, and the beloved city" (verse 9). It was mentioned earlier in this study of Revelation that one has to be careful in lining up the events brought to view in it, as in his apocalyptic style John sees first one thing, then another, and perhaps back to the first again. So it is here. "The beloved city" that John speaks of in the twentieth chapter is not mentioned earlier in the book of Revelation, and is not fully described until chapter 21. There he speaks of seeing it come down from God out of heaven. We will study it more closely in the next chapter. Obviously the city has to come down to earth before Satan and his hosts can march up against it. And it would not come down before the 1,000 years are up or it would disrupt the period in which the saints judge the world and the period in which Satan is chained. The only alternative is that the "beloved city" comes down to earth about the same time that the wicked are raised from the dead.

We have this sequence of events, then, that mark the beginning and the close of the millennium: Christ comes, the wicked are destroyed, the righteous dead are raised, they and the righteous living are taken to heaven, and thus Satan is bound. During the millennium Satan and his evil angels are confined to this desolate earth; the saints carry on a work of judgment in heaven. At the close of the millennium, the wicked are raised and thus Satan is loosed, the "beloved city" comes down to earth, and Satan marshals the wicked with the intent to besiege and capture it.

But of course they do not achieve their objective. "Fire came down from God out of heaven, and devoured them." "And death and hell were cast into the lake of fire. This is the second death" (verses 9, 14).

It may be asked, Why does God resurrect the wicked only to destroy them? Remember that God is dealing with more than people on this earth. He is dealing with more than Satan. There is a principle at stake: His nature, His name, His character. If sin is forever to be eradicated from the universe, it must be shown as without foundation, without excuse. Everyone, from the highest angel by the throne of God to the lowest demon in Satan's army, and all the people on this earth and all the creatures on every other world, must admit, freely and completely, that God is just, that there is no place for rebellion in the universe.

The first death of the wicked is not a final punishment. It is only what every son and daughter of Adam has experienced. But upon being resurrected, these wicked have the opportunity of seeing themselves in the grand scheme of things. They see the part they have played, on Satan's side in the great cosmic controversy. They see that they are without excuse. They admit that they are worthy of death, "that at the name of Jesus every knee should bow, of things in heaven, and things in earth, and things under the earth; and that every tongue should confess that Jesus Christ is Lord, to the glory of God the Father" (Philippians 2:10, 11). It is upon this confession that the way is clear at last for God to destroy the wicked and cleanse the world of sin.

This fire that destroys the wicked will do a complete work. It will "devour" them, annihilate them. "The wages of sin is death," not a continual life in a forever-burning hell (Romans 6:23). The wicked have no eternal life, no immortality. That is only for those who have Christ Jesus.

What does the Bible mean by "eternal fire"? Let the Bible explain itself. In Jude 7 we read that Sodom and Gomorrah were examples of the destruction of the wicked, that they suffered "the vengeance of eternal fire." But Sodom and Gomorrah are not burning today. They burned until there was nothing more to burn, then the fire went out. But the results of that fire are eternal. We don't expect Sodom and Gomorrah to exist again.

So it is with the punishment of the wicked. The punishment of the wicked will be eternal, for the punishment is death, and the death is eternal. But God will not be leaving a fire burning in His universe, as a gruesome reminder of the terrible blot of sin. He has gone through enough already in order to be rid of sin forever.

Satan will also be included in this eternal destruction of sin. John says, "The devil that deceived them was cast into the lake of fire and brimstone" (Revelation 20:10). Ezekiel records this pronouncement against Satan: "Thou hast defiled thy sanctuaries by the multitude of thine iniquities, by the iniquity of thy traffick; therefore will I bring forth a fire from the midst of thee, it shall devour thee, and I will bring thee to ashes upon the earth in the sight of all them that behold thee. All they that know thee among the people shall be astonished at thee: thou shalt be a terror, and *never shalt thou be any more*" (Ezekiel 28:18, 19).

This fire that consumes the wicked will purify the earth of all trace of sin. Says Peter, "The heavens shall pass away with a great noise, and the elements shall melt with fervent heat, the earth also and the works that are therein shall be burned up" (2 Peter 3:10).

But eventually the fire will go out. The wicked will be reduced to ashes (Malachi 4:1, 3). Then God will make a new beginning. "We, according to his promise, look for new heavens and a new earth, wherein dwelleth righteousness" (2 Peter 3:13). That is the good news in all this. God's original purpose for this earth when He made it and declared that it was "very good" will be accomplished at last.

the beauty it had before sin marred it—a new Garden of Eden, if you please. Isaiah tries to describe the change in human terms: "The wilderness and the solitary place shall be glad for them; and the desert shall rejoice, and blossom as the rose." "In the wilderness shall waters break out, and streams in the desert. And the parched ground shall become a pool, and the thirsty land springs of water" (Isaiah 35:1, 6, 7).

Especially will the people of God find the restored earth to their satisfaction. The saints will be able to recognize one another, for they will have real bodies, even as Adam had a real body in the first Eden, and as Jesus had a real body after His resurrection. But those bodies will not be subject to disease or harm, and the marks of suffering in this present life will have been obliterated.

"Then the eyes of the blind shall be opened, and the ears of the deaf shall be unstopped. Then shall the lame man leap as an hart, and the tongue of the dumb sing." "And the ransomed of the Lord shall return, and come to Zion with songs and everlasting joy upon their heads: they shall obtain joy and gladness, and sorrow and sighing shall flee away" (verses 5, 6, 10).

It is of this time that the famous promise is given, "The wolf also shall dwell with the lamb, and the leopard shall lie down with the kid; and the calf and the young lion and the fatling together; and a little child shall lead them. . . . They shall not hurt nor destroy in all my holy mountain: for the earth shall be full of the knowledge of the Lord, as the waters cover the sea" (Isaiah 11:6-9).

Referring to the frequency with which people make plans but cannot carry them out, or build only to see another enjoy the fruit of their labors, Isaiah says, "They shall build houses, and inhabit them; and they shall plant vineyards, and eat the fruit of them. They shall not build, and another inhabit; they shall not plant, and another eat: for as the days of a tree are the days of my people, and mine elect shall long enjoy the work of their hands" (Isaiah 65:21, 22). Certainly there will be no plant disease then, nor pests, nor rot or ruin of any kind, for all these are the consequences of sin.

The prophet who recorded all these promises also speaks of the capital city of this brand-new world: "Behold, I create new heavens and a new earth: and the former shall not be remembered, nor come into mind. But be ye glad and rejoice for ever in that which I create: for, behold, I create Jerusalem a rejoicing, and her people a joy" (verses 17, 18).

That brings us back to John and the book of Revelation. The prophet says, "I John saw the holy city, new Jerusalem, coming down from God out of heaven, prepared as a bride adorned for her husband" (Revelation 21:2). Surely this is the city of "many mansions" that Jesus told His disciples He would go to prepare (John 14:2). It is the city that Abraham looked for, "a city which hath foundations [that would have a lot of meaning to a wandering nomad such as Abraham], whose builder and maker is God" (Hebrews 11:10).

John was given a close-up view of the city. He tries to describe it for us, but we should remember that, as a heavenly place, as the special creation of God for His people, the city in reality probably far surpasses John's description. When John tried to describe his vision of God, he could give only an approximation of majesty (Revelation 4:3). And so, although the city John saw is real, its qualities would be difficult for a human being to fathom.

For example, John says an angel measured the

city." "The Spirit and the bride say, Come. . . . And let him that is athirst come. And whosoever will, let him take the water of life freely" (Revelation 22:6, 7, 13, 14, 17).

"Even so, come, Lord Jesus" (verse 20). That was John's closing prayer, and I hereby make it mine. Won't you join me?